D

22|

Praise for Maude Julien and *The Only Girl in the World*

'A living testimony of resilience…An account as gripping as it is inspiring.' *Elle*

'Maude Julien delivers a staggering testimony, one that remains full of hope.' *Ouest-France*

'A serious subject: manipulation, in which the author is now a professional therapist. Maude Julien does not write with resentment, or bear grievances— she delivers a clear message of hope.' *Livres Hebdo*

'Once you read *The Only Girl in the World*, you wonder: how on earth can this have happened, and how can the product of this conditioning have managed to integrate into society? You'd expect an agoraphobic, a traumatised madwoman…Whereas Maude Julien exudes vitality.' *Libération*

'Despite appearances, this is not the umpteenth book about a miraculously saved victim. It is much more, and much better…One of the most fascinating things about this book is the extraordinary resistance that Maude developed…her ability to develop a world for herself.' *Le Journal du Dimanche*

'This story is never maudlin—it is so absorbing that you have to remind yourself to breathe from time to time.' *Le Point*

'Her book offers a ray of hope.' *Metro Belgique*

MAUDE JULIEN works as a psychotherapist, specialising in mind and behavioural control, emotional manipulation and trauma, and conducts anthropological research among Indigenous Australians. She lives in Paris.

URSULA GAUTHIER is a journalist at the French weekly magazine *L'Obs*, and the author and co-author of many works. She lives in Paris.

ADRIANA HUNTER is the prize-winning translator of works by writers including Catherine Millet, Amélie Nothomb and Véronique Olmi.

The Only Girl in the World

A MEMOIR

By **Maude Julien**

With **Ursula Gauthier**

TRANSLATED BY ADRIANA HUNTER

ONEWORLD

A Oneworld Book

First published in Great Britain and the Republic of Ireland
by Oneworld Publications, 2018

First published in France by Editions Stock in 2014 under the title *Derrière la grille*

ISBN 978-1-78607-135-4
ISBN 978-1-78607-136-1 (ebook)

Typeset by J&M Typesetting
Printed and bound in Great Britain Clays Ltd, St Ives plc

Oneworld Publications
10 Bloomsbury Street
London WC1B 3SR
United Kingdom

Stay up to date with the latest books,
special offers, and exclusive content from
Oneworld with our monthly newsletter

Sign up on our website
oneworld-publications.com

MIX
Paper from
responsible sources
FSC® C018072

TO MY MOTHER,
the first victim of the Ogre

INTRODUCTION

In 1936, Louis Didier was thirty-four and financially well-off. A man from humble origins, he had risen remarkably quickly through the ranks of French society and he now ran a company in Lille. Initiated into an esoteric lodge of Freemasonry, he adhered to an extremely dark spiritual vision of a fallen world governed by grim forces.

That year he met a man, a miner from the town of Fives, who was struggling to feed his many children. Louis Didier suggested the miner 'entrust' to him his youngest child, a flaxen-haired six-year-old girl. 'Jeannine will never want for anything; she will have a brilliant education and enjoy a very comfortable life. My only condition is that you will no longer see her.'

It's unclear whether there was a financial transaction. The

miner agreed. Jeannine left to live under Louis Didier's protection and never saw her family again.

Louis Didier kept his promise. Jeannine was sent to boarding school and received an excellent education. When she reached the age of consent, she came back to live with her guardian. He had her study philosophy and Latin at university in Lille, and made sure she earned her degree.

I don't know when Louis Didier revealed his grand project to Jeannine. Did he talk about it when she was still a little girl who spent only holidays with him? Or did he wait until she'd grown up and become his wife? I think that deep down Jeannine 'always knew' what her mission was: to give him a daughter as blonde as she was, and then to take charge of the child's education.

Louis believed that the child Jeannine brought into the world would be, like her father, 'chosen'—and that later in life she would be called upon to 'raise up humanity'. Thanks to her mother's qualifications, this child would be raised away from the polluting influences of the outside world. Louis Didier would be responsible for training her physically and mentally to become a 'superior being', equipped to undertake the difficult and momentous task he had assigned her.

Twenty-two years after he took possession of Jeannine, Louis Didier decided the time had come for her to bring his daughter into the world and that the date of birth should be November 23rd, 1957.

On November 23rd, 1957, Jeannine gave birth to a very blonde little girl.

Three years later, aged fifty-nine, Louis Didier liquidated his assets, bought a house near Cassel, between Lille and Dunkirk, and withdrew to live there with Jeannine in order to devote himself entirely to carrying out the project he had devised back in 1936: to make his child a superhuman being.

That child was me.

Linda

When I first come to the house I'm not yet four. I'm wearing a red coat. I can still feel its texture against my fingers, thick and felted. I'm not holding anyone's hand and there's no one beside me. I can just feel my fists bunched in my pockets, gripping the fabric, clinging to it.

There's lots of brown gravel on the ground. I hate this place. The garden seems to go on forever; I feel like it's swallowing me up. And then there's that dark, disturbing structure: a huge house looming to my right.

I hear the heavy gate scraping along the gravel as it closes behind me. A screeching *creak-creak-creak* until the two sides of the gate clang together. Then comes the *click* of the lock, followed by a *clunk*: the gate is shut for good. I don't dare turn around. It feels like a lid has just been closed over me.

Whenever the two of us are alone, my mother tells me it's my fault we had to leave Lille and bury ourselves in this hole. That I'm not normal. I have to be hidden, otherwise I'd be locked up in Bailleul straightaway. Bailleul is the lunatic asylum. I went there once, when my parents took on one of their inmates as a maid. It's a terrifying place, filled with screams and commotion.

It's true, I'm not really normal. In Lille I had terrible tantrums during which I slammed my head against the walls. I was a bundle of indomitable will, full of joy and rage. It hurt when the uneven surface of the walls dug into my head, when my mother crushed my hand in hers and dragged me away by the arm. But I wasn't afraid. I felt brave, nothing could break me.

My father had the walls coated with a roughcast of an even coarser texture in order to 'tame' me. It didn't do any good. I still went and hit my head against those walls in fits of anger. I had to have my head stitched up so many times that my scalp is littered with scars. My mother, who would graze herself or tear her dresses against the walls as she walked past, was furious with me.

Since we've been in this house, I don't feel as strong. I'm alone. I don't go to nursery school anymore. My mother teaches me now, up on the second floor. I no longer go to my father's garage, where the workmen used to make me laugh. We hardly ever go out and we have very few visitors.

What I want is to go to school, proper school, where I can have a teacher and lots of friends. Even though I'm terrified of my father, I ask, 'Can I go back to school one day?' and my parents look at me as if I've just uttered something outrageous. My mother seems disgusted. My father's eyes bore into mine. 'Don't you realize,' he says, 'that it's for your sake I've put your mother through all these years of studying? She had a hell of a time, believe me. She thought she'd never succeed. And I made her keep going. With the qualifications she has, she could teach a whole class. But you have her all to yourself until you take your *baccalauréat* at eighteen. You have such good fortune and still you complain?'

I don't know what demon prompts me with this ill-advised idea: 'If she can teach an entire class, couldn't we have a class with some other pupils?' An icy silence ensues. My limbs freeze. I know I won't dare broach the subject again. I won't be going to school.

Luckily for me there's Linda. She came to the house at about the same time as us. We grew up together. In my oldest memories of her, she's not yet fully grown. When she wags her tail it brushes my face. It tickles. It makes me laugh. I like the smell of her coat.

While she's a puppy she sleeps in the kitchen because the nights are cold in northern France. But she's not allowed into any of the other rooms. When we're in the dining room, I can hear her whining down the corridor. She's soon exiled to the unheated utility room.

My father can't wait to put her well and truly outside. He has a painted wooden kennel delivered and puts it in the garden behind the kitchen. That's where Linda has to sleep now. She's absolutely forbidden from coming into the house—until a serious cold snap comes along, which brings the poor, shivering creature back into the utility room, her hair matted with ice.

My father is annoyed. 'Dogs are for guarding the house,' he says. 'They belong outside.' The cold spell ends, and Linda spends more and more time tied to the railings on the outside steps. That's where I go to see her at every opportunity. She looks huge to me. I take her by the collar and bury my face in her fur. My father, who bellows orders at her, terrifies her. My mother, whom Linda views with cool courtesy, is exasperated. 'That dog's mine,' she keeps telling me. 'But of course you have to own everything. You act as if she's yours. And you've managed to make the stupid animal believe it herself.'

I feel ashamed. I don't understand who belongs to whom. Linda couldn't care less, though. She continues to jump all over me in delight.

One day some builders come. My father tells me that Linda is going to have a palace. I'm ecstatic for her. When it's built, this 'palace' is a strange shape: the first part is high enough for an adult to stand upright, then there's a lower area insulated with glass wool 'to keep her nice and warm'. From now on Linda can stay outside no matter the weather.

Strangely, Linda refuses point blank to set foot in the back part of the kennel. My father tells me to go and sit at the far end so she'll get used to it, and Linda soon comes to join me. For several days we have fun sneaking into the little alcove and snuggling up together.

A week later, my father calls for me in the middle of the afternoon, and orders me to go to the kennel with the dog. Hurray! An unexpected break from lessons! Linda races over to me, thrilled, and we curl up together in our little refuge. I think that's when I hear the workmen come over. I don't know why my heart constricts. They come into the kennel carrying a heavy metal gate with black and white painted bars. They lift it up and—*clank*—they set it onto hinges.

'Maude, get out of there!' my father yells. I obey him. I have no choice but to obey. I come out, leaving Linda behind the bars, her eyes full of sad incomprehension. 'You see,' my father says, looking me squarely in the eye, 'she trusted you and look where that got her. You must never trust anyone.'

From that day until the end of her life, Linda is locked in her kennel from eight in the morning until eight at night. She trusted me and I didn't see it coming. She is trapped because of me.

At first, Linda whines, scratches at the bars, and reaches out a paw when I walk by. I'm not allowed to stop. I look at her, word-lessly apologizing. As the weeks pass, she takes to sitting behind her gate in complete silence, the spark fading from her eyes, just wagging her tail when she sees me.

Then her character changes. She starts having aggressive outbursts and no one knows what triggers them. She growls and bares her teeth when she hears footsteps. After eight in the evening, when she's free to run in the garden, she even chases my mother. She's a big German shepherd and she can be very menacing when she wants. My mother defends herself by throwing buckets of water at her. Linda takes to shaking at the very sight of a bucket.

My father is satisfied. Linda has become quite a good guard dog. To fine-tune her training, he sometimes lets her out of her prison and tells her to guard his bicycle. She has to sit motionless next to it. He then makes me walk up to her, and as soon as she wags her tail he shouts. She immediately tucks her tail between her legs. Once she understands how to guard the bike, he pats her and rewards her with a couple of hours of freedom.

After a few months of this training, he decides to test her. When Linda is sitting stiff as a board, standing guard next to the bike, my father tells me to run over, snatch the bike and take it away. I do as I'm told. Seeing me running towards her, Linda jumps to her feet, leaps at me and sinks her canines into the flesh of my thigh. I scream in surprise and pain. Linda immediately lets go and lies flat on the ground, gazing at me with desperate eyes. 'Absolutely anyone, no matter what stupid orders they're under, will attack you—even this dog who you think is so faithful to you,' my father says.

I still love Linda just as much; I'll never believe she bit me deliberately. It was just an accident. My father often returns to this episode. He wants me to understand that he's the only one who loves and protects me. That I should trust only him.

Pitou

Every evening at eight o'clock, I go and release Linda from her prison. Before letting her out into the garden for the night, I quietly tell her stories, and she listens attentively. I don't want anyone to hear what I'm telling her, so I whisper in her ear. Sometimes it tickles her and she rubs her ear against my cheek. I often tell her about the ducks that live by the pond my father had dug at the bottom of the garden.

It's migration season, and wild ducks are flying overhead. Some of them occasionally land in the grounds of our house. My father worries because our animals might be 'polluted' by these outsiders. He takes out his shotgun and fires at the intruders. My mother drives them out by pumping a big brown bellows at them, making an unbearable trumpeting noise.

We have to stop our own birds from trying to escape, so we

clip one wing on each of them. I'm the one who has to catch them, because for some inexplicable reason, they readily come to me. It breaks my heart to see how quickly they come when I call. I hand them to my mother one at a time, and she toils away at removing their feathers with chunky scissors. Duck feathers are very tough. She crops them very short, sometimes so short she draws blood. All our ducks have a ridiculous waddle, their intact wing looking huge compared to the stump on the other side.

I tell Linda about the hideous crunch of the scissors on their feathers, the smell of the droppings they release out of fear. I feel like the ducks on the pond, with one wing that my parents want long and beautiful and the other cut to the quick.

Thankfully I also have some more cheerful stories to tell her. Like the one about Pitou, a Barbary duckling we managed to save from certain death. Pitou was quacking pitifully. The three of us ran over and spotted him, a pathetic tuft of feathers, pinioned under a big drake who kept driving the little one's head underwater with his beak. The drake must have been his own father, intent on drowning him.

My mother grabs a stick and hits at the big drake to get him to let go of Pitou. But he's tough; he dodges the blows without letting go. She doesn't either. She runs along the narrow pontoon across the pond. And splash, she falls in. I lean over to reach out my hand, and I fall in too. 'How the hell did I end up with such a pair of idiots!' my father shouts, exasperated. We splash about in the filthy, stinking water; my mother's chignon comes undone and her long blond hair trails through the sludge. Finally, she grabs me by the collar and lifts me onto the pontoon.

I'm covered in mud, but I can't abandon Pitou. He has

11

succeeded in escaping from his father but is struggling helplessly, about to drown. I lean forward again and manage to grab him. Then my foot slips and I end up back in the water. By clutching onto the pontoon I haul myself onto the bank at last, without letting go of Pitou.

The poor thing shivers in my hands, his wet feathers clinging to his sides. 'He's freezing!' I cry. 'He's going to die of cold!' My father, who was overcome by rage only moments earlier, suddenly softens. Does Pitou remind him of the rabbit he loved as a child and that his father, a heartless man, had served at the dinner table one evening? 'You'll just have to put him in the oven to warm up,' he grunts.

Overjoyed, I run to the kitchen. Once Pitou is dry, I keep him with me the rest of the day, and every day after that. My father definitely has a soft spot for him. He lets me take him every-where, comfortably nestled in a box filled with cotton wool.

A few days later the honeymoon is over, and I have to take Pitou back to the duck pen. But his father is still just as hostile: as soon as he sees Pitou, he lunges at him, hitting him with his beak. I ask my father if Pitou can live outside the fence around the pond. 'If you like,' he says, 'but when Linda eats him, you'll only have yourself to blame.' Pitou shows absolutely no fear of Linda. He wanders freely around the garden except for the area by the pond, which he avoids like the plague. Despite my efforts to teach him to swim, he struggles like a thing possessed and makes pathetic noises as soon as I take him near water.

Pitou grows into a handsome black duck with a red head. Whenever he sees me, he comes waddling over. He stays right by my side while I'm working in the grounds of the property and makes me laugh with his peals of exuberant quacking. He's lucky that he's a Barbary duck, which means he can't fly: he doesn't need to have his wing clipped like the others. But the thing that makes me really happy is that he gets on very well with Linda. When she's locked up during the day, he slips between the bars and joins her in the back of the kennel.

Linda and Pitou are my darlings, I'd do anything for them. My parents understand this. If they want me to do something, they need only say, 'Watch out! If you don't do it, Linda will be locked up for two extra hours a day for a month,' or 'We'll put Pitou in a wooden crate for three days with nothing to eat or drink' or, worse still, 'We'll put Pitou back where he belongs'— that is, the pond, where I know he wouldn't survive. So my minor rebellion instantly dissolves.

My father often mentions the story of Pitou when he's teaching me about human nature. 'If you go and live with other humans, they'll treat you the way the ducks in the pond treat Pitou. They won't think twice about making mincemeat of you for the stupidest reasons, or for no reason at all.'

Lindbergh

My father doesn't like me doing nothing. When I was little, I was allowed to play in the garden once I'd finished studying. But now that I'm almost five, I have less free time. 'You mustn't waste your time,' my father says. 'Focus on your duties.'

In spite of everything, my mind sometimes wanders, and I sit there staring into space. Or when there's construction work to do on the grounds, I might stop to catch my breath. And then, without fail, this horrible silence descends on me. My heart starts pounding. I turn around slowly, and there he is behind me, standing bolt upright. 'What are you doing?' he roars. I'm helpless: I can't open my mouth, which makes me look guilty, I know. Overwhelmed with fear, I feverishly go back to work.

I don't know how he does it, but my father has a sixth sense when it comes to my weaknesses. The minute I relax, I know he's there, right behind me, with his piercing eyes. Even when he's not there in the flesh, I can feel his eyes boring into the back of my head.

When my mother and I are clearing undergrowth on the grounds, I admire a marvellous tree out of the corner of my eye. It's not the biggest or the fullest, but it's the most beautiful. It has a big, low-hanging branch which sticks out horizontally from the trunk, then gracefully curves around before heading skyward. I dream of sitting in the crook of that curve, which looks as if it was made for a child to play in. One day, when my mother was some distance away, I sat in delight on that low branch. I don't remember how long I stayed there. But I clearly remember my father's hand violently pulling my hair from behind and throwing me to the ground so sharply that it knocked the breath out of me. I didn't hear him approach. Ever since then, I settle for gazing from afar at the tree of happiness.

I don't have much free time, anyway. Between schoolwork, music, my share of the housework, and serving my father, my days are very full. I can sometimes sneak into the big room which looks out onto the street. I watch passers-by for a few minutes. I try to go there in the mornings, at about eight o'clock, before lessons with my mother. That's when the workmen head to the Cathelain factory, just on the other side of the grounds. They walk briskly past the house, carrying their lunch in pails. Occasionally I manage to see them in the evenings too, around six o'clock. They look tired as they head home, but I can tell they're happy. Occasionally I see a woman waiting for them along the way, or a child running to greet them. I look at those faces. At night, in bed, I picture myself later in life, married to a factory worker who sets off in the mornings with a pail filled with a meal I've made for him.

In the mornings I also see children on their way to school, in groups or pairs. It seems extraordinary to me, this heading off to school. I dream of having to do that. Of course, my 'school' is on the second floor. I summon all my courage and bring it up with my mother: I suggest that I could go out of the gate on the grounds, as if I too were heading off to school, then come back along the fence to the front door. My mother listens without a word.

A little later I'm summoned to the dining room. My parents look very serious, as usual. My father starts talking about the famous American aviator Charles Lindbergh, whom he met when he was young. He is one of the few living people he respects. They have a lot in common. To start with, they were both born in 1902. Like Lindbergh, my father was an aviator and, like him, he is a very high-ranking Freemason. Charles Lindbergh had a son, a baby who was kidnapped and killed. This was the 'crime of the century' and it had a profound effect on my father. Does he make it clear to me that this happened a long time ago, before the war? Regardless, his solemn tone makes such an impression that I think the tragedy has only just happened. My heart aches for this poor Charles Lindbergh.

Now my mother chimes in. 'The Peugeots' son was also kidnapped,' she says. I don't know exactly when this happened, but imagine it's very recent as well. Luckily, the child was saved, but he'd nevertheless faced terrible danger. My father has connections with the Peugeots too, because for a long time he owned the largest Peugeot car dealership in Lille.

'You're in danger, too,' he says, looking at me intently. 'People will try to abduct you. That's why you mustn't go out. It would only take one car—like the black 403 that snatched little Eric Peugeot—to drive past you, and you'd vanish with your kidnappers.'

He reminds me of another safety measure I already know well: the lights must never be switched on when the shutters are open, because this would make us easy targets for a potential sniper hiding on the other side of the road. First the shutters have to be rolled down using the crank handle, and only then can the lights go on.

I'm given to understand that there's a 'wave of child kidnappings' going on at the moment. After the Lindbergh baby and the Peugeot boy, I'm third on the list. I must look very frightened because my father takes the trouble to reassure me. He tells me I'm lucky to have scars 'marking both sides of my body' so I don't run the risk of becoming a victim of the 'white slave trade'. And these scars would certainly help my father recognize me in any circumstances. My trust in him should never waver.

My mother endorses this: 'Monsieur Didier can do everything and see everything.' I don't know whether I feel reassured or terrified.

My father reiterates the fact that everything he does is for me. That he devotes his entire life to me, to training me, shaping me, sculpting me into the superior being I'm destined to become. He tells me he has loved me since long before I was born. He has always wanted to have a daughter he would call Maude. Maude with an 'e', like the wife of Robin Hood's sidekick, Will Scarlet. An exceptional woman, a warrior, an Amazon, faithful to her love

17

until she dies. He tells me he dreamed of me even when he was very young. And as soon as he could, he did what needed to be done in order to bring me into the world. It was a lengthy undertaking. First he had to find the woman who would give birth to me. He found my mother, who was only five or six when he chose her. She was the youngest child of a northern mining family and he was already a very rich man, so he had no trouble convincing her parents to entrust her to him. He kept her away from her family to protect her from outside influences. He threw himself heart and soul into bringing her up and giving her the best education possible, and then when the time came, she gave birth to me.

I need to understand just how much my very existence is a result of my father's plans. I know I must prove worthy of the tasks he will set for me later. But I'm afraid I won't measure up to his vision. I feel too feeble, too clumsy, too stupid. And I'm so frightened of him. The sheer heft of him, his big head, his long thin hands and his steely eyes—I'm so terrified my legs give way when I come close to him.

I'm all the more horrified because I'm alone against this titan. I can expect no comfort or protection from my mother. 'Monsieur Didier' is a demigod to her, one she both adores and loathes, but would never dare to oppose. I have no other choice but to close my eyes and, shaking with fear, put myself under my creator's wing.

My father is convinced that the mind can achieve anything. Absolutely anything: it can overcome every danger and conquer every obstacle. But to do this requires long, rigorous training away from the impurities of this dirty world. He's always saying, 'Man is profoundly evil, the world is profoundly dangerous. The

18

earth is full of weak, cowardly people driven to treachery by their weakness and cowardice.' My father has been disappointed by the world; he has often been betrayed. 'You don't know how lucky you are to be spared from being polluted by other people,' he tells me. That's what the house is for, to keep the miasma of the outside world at arm's length.

He sometimes tells me that I should never leave the house, even after he's dead. His memory will live on here, and if I watch over it, I'll be safe. Other times he informs me that later, I'll be able to do whatever I want, that I could be President of France, master of the world. But when I leave the house, it won't be to live a pointless life as 'Mrs Nobody'. It will be to conquer the world and 'achieve greatness'. I'll have to come back from time to time to recharge myself 'at home base': in other words, in this house, which absorbs more and more of my father's power every day.

There is also a third possible scenario: for me to stay at the house to put into practice the lessons in discipline he has been drilling into me since childhood. And to prepare myself for the day when I'm called upon to 'raise up humanity'. I ask him how I'll know when it's time to raise up humanity. 'I'll let you know, even if I'm no longer here.'

When I think of my secret dreams of a factory-worker husband and his lunch pail, I feel ashamed.

To avoid disappointing him too much I wage war on my many faults. But there's one I just can't control: I have a habit of twitching my nose and mouth and screwing up my eyes. 'Stop making faces,' my mother often says. My father hates it. Since I was little he has made me sit facing him 'without moving a muscle'.

At first I had to stay still for a few minutes. Then a quarter of an hour. Once I turn five, he adds what he calls 'the impassivity tests' to my daily schedule, between eight and eight-fifteen in the evening. Then the sessions become even longer and are held at any time of day, sometimes lasting several hours and delaying my lessons and homework, which then all have to be caught up. And now my mother has to do them too—when we're alone she's quick to tell me how much she resents me for this.

'You mustn't reveal anything with your face or your body,' my father says in his deep voice, 'otherwise you'll be eaten alive. Only weak people have facial expressions. You need to learn to control yourself if you want to be a great poker player.'

Do I want to be a great poker player? I don't know, I've never played poker. But I have to be ready in case I ever need to later. At various difficult times in his life, my father pulled through thanks to his skill at poker. He was able to appear perfectly neutral while reading his adversaries' body language and facial expressions like a book.

The hardest part of these impassivity tests is the itching. It's there right from the start, tickling in every direction. It stops after a while. Then it starts up again even worse and becomes pure torment. The one who really can't cope is my mother. There always comes a point when one of her arms or legs shoots up as if on a spring. It takes enormous effort not to burst out laughing. 'Your mother has St Vitus's Dance,' my father spits with utter contempt, still scrutinizing the mirror in front of me to check I haven't moved so much as an eyelash. He views 'St Vitus's Dance' as a hallmark of the weak and inept.

I'm afraid I'm weak and inept too. Playing chess with my father is torture. I have to sit very upright on the edge of my

20

chair and respect the rules of impassivity while I consider my next move. I can feel myself dissolving under his stare. When I move a pawn he asks sarcastically, 'Have you really thought about what you're doing?' I panic and want to move the pawn back. He doesn't allow it: 'You've touched the piece, now you have to follow through. Think before you act. Think.'

Kennedy

I'm in my mother's room, in pyjamas. She's dictating a strange letter to me; it starts: 'My darling little Daddy' and includes 'I love you' many times. Ever since I've known how to write, my mother has dictated 'Happy Mother's Day' and 'Happy Father's Day' letters to me. Not knowing the exact dates, she decided Mother's Day fell on the third Sunday in May, and Father's Day, on the third Sunday in June.

I don't say anything, but I always think this is very strange. We never use terms of endearment because they're 'for the weak and sappy'. The word 'darling', for instance, is never said in our house. Writing 'My darling little Mummy' feels even more bizarre, given her tone of voice when she dictates the words. In actual fact, my mother loathes my name and goes out of her way never to utter it. And I make sure I never call her 'Mummy'.

Because they're a 'present', the writing time for these letters is taken out of my allocated sleep time. At bedtime she makes me sit on the footstool at her dressing table, which makes it quite difficult to write neatly. Usually, when I make an inkblot with my pen, she gets hysterical and has me start over, ten times if need be. But on these occasions the quality of my writing doesn't matter. If I don't know how to spell a word, she says, 'Write it however you like.' That's also odd. She normally hits me over the head with a ruler if I make a spelling mistake.

Sometimes what she dictates makes me laugh to myself. Like today, when the letter ends with 'I hope I'll have a husband like you when I'm older.' A complete lie. If I have a husband when I'm older, I hope he'll be like the Cathelain factory workers, and not like my father. Last year, I had to write: 'I'd never want any other daddy but you.' Can you choose your own father?

When I've finished writing my 'Happy Mother's Day' letter, she dismisses me without a kiss. In our house, we never touch, even on Mother's Day. I have to go back to my room and wait till she's in bed before slipping my letter under the door. The next morning, she shows it to my father, saying, 'Look what I found when I woke up this morning.' The letter to my father has to be slipped under his door one day before Father's Day: to prove I haven't forgotten the date.

I don't understand these letters at all, like plenty of other things. But I don't ask questions. The only answer I'd get would be: 'There are rules and you have to follow them. Stop asking stupid questions.'

The waking-up rule is one example. My bedroom is separated from my mother's by her bathroom. At six-thirty every morning she opens my door—*wham!*—and she flicks the light on and yells, 'Get up!' My mother thinks people who get up at seven are 'slackers'. Under her watchful eye, I have to get straight out of bed and dress in less than two minutes. Then she says, 'Go and wake your father and see how he's doing.'

Everything is always exactly the same each morning. The only variation is that my mother sometimes says, 'see if he's in a good mood' instead of 'see how he's doing'.

But this morning is different. Something's wrong. She goes back to her room as soon as she's put the light on. I dress as quickly as possible to avoid getting cold. Then I wait, not sure what to do. If I don't go and wake my father, I'll get in trouble. But if I go when she hasn't told me to, I'll get in trouble too. I rack my brains, trying to remember whether they said anything yesterday evening…In the end, I decide it would be better to go and knock on my father's door.

Is the change in routine because it's my birthday today? As far as my father is concerned, birthdays are not celebrations, and I have to be trained so that mine never becomes one. Which is why every November 23rd I have a longer school day and no recess. I'm waiting anxiously to know what the new 'teaching' for my sixth birthday will be.

We are in the dining room. My mother and I are standing in front of my father, who is looking daggers at us. I've never seen my mother so afraid. She stammers something about someone who's been killed and how his wife threw herself over him and how it's 'the end of the world'. My father barks at me in his stentorian voice: 'How did she know? How did she find out?' I'm terrified. I have no idea what he's talking about. How did she know what? My throat feels tight, not a sound comes out. He accuses me of 'covering for' my mother, then turns to her and bombards her with questions: 'How did you find out? Who told you about Kennedy? How do you know he's been assassinated? Answer me, you idiot! Answer!'

Someone's been assassinated? Who? Is the body in the house? And why does my mother keep saying we'll soon have a third world war?

Eventually she cracks and admits that she secretly listens to the radio. My father is beside himself. 'Where is this radio? Go and find it!' he bellows at me. I'm rooted to the spot; all I know is I mustn't cry. Then my mother comes up behind me and knees me in the back, saying between gritted teeth, 'See what happens on your birthday!' She goes back upstairs and reappears carrying an old radio with big dials. My father sends me to get a hammer from the cellar and then tells my mother: 'Jeannine, give it a really good whack.'

That night I hear my mother crying in her room. I feel guilty; I did something terrible and someone has died because of me. I start wondering whether my father really is my father or if he is actually my mother's father. I tell myself the man who's been assassinated is her real husband. Which makes him my real father, and he might have died trying to help us. I lie there in bed, heavy-hearted and shivering in the cold.

One question plagues me: who are my mother's real parents? I realize I have absolutely no idea. My mother never talks about them. My father is not very talkative either, but, for my edification, he does occasionally tell me about his tough, impoverished childhood. As a boy, he had to slip between the bars of gates or into basements to steal things that his father then sold in his grocery store. His father was a harsh man who beat him hard. My father also talks about the bombings during World War I. He was twelve in 1914 and experienced true famine; he even had to eat rats. He mentions his mother less frequently and, when he does, his voice starts to tremble.

My mother, though, never has anything to say about her childhood. When I ask her, 'Who is your mother and where is she?' she gives me only crumbs of information. I gradually piece together that she was born into a mining family in Fives, in the north. There were seven or eight children, all girls except for one boy. 'They're not educated or intelligent,' she says.

I ask her why she left them. 'One day,' she tells me, 'my eldest sister Henriette came home with your father. At the time, he looked very tall and frightening to me. They took me to his house. I didn't know I'd never go back home to my parents, but when I figured it out, I didn't miss them.' She was sent away to boarding school very young, and was extremely happy there. Then she went to university so that she'd be able to home-school me when the time came.

'I was six when your father came to take me away,' she says. 'The same age you are now. You see, I mean as much to him as you do.' It's as if a light has suddenly appeared at the end of a tunnel. 'What about me? Now that I'm six, will someone come to take me away too?' I ask hopefully. 'We've done all this for you,' she answers icily, 'and you don't understand anything. You always want to leave. If you say that to your father, you'll kill him. And it will be all your fault.'

Madame Descombes

In my father's opinion, music is more important than any other subject. He and my mother aren't musicians so they enrol me in a correspondence course. I can already name the notes as I sing and read all the keys. I'm studying sharps and flats, and major and minor keys. It's time I start learning to play an instrument. At first my parents want me to study the piano by correspondence, but they eventually concede that this isn't very practical.

That's how Madame Descombes comes into my life. My parents choose her because she teaches piano at the conservatory in Lille and used to be a concert pianist. She's an older lady, tiny and thin with short grey hair, which I think is very beautiful. I've never seen a woman with short hair before. She asks me if I can play anything. 'I can do some scales,' I say shyly.

'Good. Play me a scale in C major.'

To her astonishment, I play the scale in the correct order with my right hand but in the wrong order with my left. 'Who on earth taught you that?' she exclaims. My mother is sitting in on this first lesson so I don't dare say she was the one who 'explained' how I should play a scale, based on the lesson sent to us. 'I did, with the lesson notes,' I stammer. 'If you don't know something,' Madame Descombes says sternly, 'you have to find out! You should have asked your mother.'

Twice a month my parents drive me to her house, not far from Lille. Every time I am filled with anguish. First of all, there's the memory of that excruciating first lesson. I'm ashamed that I claimed I could play when I couldn't. There's also the fear that I haven't properly grasped the last lesson and may have done my exercises wrong. But I'm also very glad to be seeing her again. She quickly sets my scales right and teaches me how to recognize all the keys.

When she shows me how to play a piece, hearing her play so well makes my heart pound. She's a strict and demanding teacher, but she's fair. She puts five-franc pieces on the backs of my hands to keep them perfectly flat when I play. If I make a mistake, she raps me over the fingers with her ruler. But she never hurts my spirit, she only hits me to correct my mistakes. I know the rule and we both respect it. She never confides anything or pays me any compliments. But I adore Madame Descombes and I get the impression she's pleased with my progress.

We sit at a beautiful baby grand piano, in front of a picture painted by her daughter. Madame Descombes once told me her daughter had never taken any interest in music. She preferred art so she chose to become a painter. I look at the painting and can't understand how she could 'choose'. We do things because we have to.

Madame Descombes can't bear musicians who pull faces when they're playing. If I ever frown or bite my lip, she takes a mirror from her bag and puts it in front of me. 'We're not at the circus here, you're not a monkey entertaining the crowd with your grimacing. You're interpreting a score, and it's your playing that should carry the expression, not your face.'

Another thing Madame Descombes can't stand is injured hands. She scolds me when she sees the scratches on my skin. I lower my head. I don't dare tell her my father has started more construction work. We're cementing the cellar floors this year. As usual, he's asked the two workmen, Albert and Rémi, to use me as a 'labourer' for two two-hour stints every day. 'To learn the harsh realities of life.' So I have to shift wheelbarrow loads of sand, turn the cement mixer and carry bricks by hand. And I'm strictly forbidden from wearing protective gloves.

One day, when the tips of my fingers are sore and bleeding, she gets angry. 'That's enough, I'm going to have words with your parents. They need to stop.' How did she know? When the lesson is over I hear her talking to my mother. 'You know how important a pianist's hands are,' she says. 'And anyway, it isn't normal for a little girl's fingers to be in that state.' She's determined to come downstairs and discuss the matter with my father, who is waiting in the car. 'Listen,' my mother says, stopping her. 'My husband's not well, we need to leave. But I promise I'll talk to him about it.' Madame Descombes adds that I'm making progress: 'She's a gifted child, you really should enrol her at the conservatory where she can prepare properly for exams and competitions.'

I immediately picture myself setting off for the conservatory with Madame Descombes, meeting other musicians there, and working hard. I'll do anything to make her proud.

This isn't the first time Madame Descombes has mentioned the conservatory. But my mother never says a word about it. 'Everything okay?' my father asks before starting the car. My mother just says yes. I try to bring up the conservatory, but she interrupts me: 'Be quiet, that's all nonsense,' she snaps. 'What is?' my father asks. 'Oh, nothing, I'll explain later,' she tells him.

For a long time after that, I imagine I hear someone ringing the doorbell: Madame Descombes has come to see my father and insists that I must go to the conservatory. In actual fact, I never see her again, or hear another word about her. My parents say nothing and I don't dare ask. It's as if she never existed.

None of which means I stop playing the piano. My father decides that from now on Yves, my accordion teacher, will give me piano lessons too. Yves conducts a small band that plays at local dances. He's an excellent musician who can play Liszt and Chopin, but his mood swings terrify me.

As a child, Yves was taught the accordion the hard way, strapped to his chair for twelve hours a day by his father. This turned him into a virtuoso player, but an appalling teacher. Thin, and a chain-smoker, he fidgets around me as I play. At the tiniest mistake, he cuffs me and hurls insults at me. He shouts so much I can't even understand what I did wrong.

Sometimes he's not so on edge, but that's even more worrying. On these occasions when he wants to punish me, he throws his beer in my face. Or he stubs out his cigarette on my thigh. I'm so tense that my playing goes from bad to worse. The punishments come thick and fast. During my first piano lesson, he's obviously surprised by the quality of my playing, which is mainly thanks to Madame Descombes. 'How come you play so well, when you're so hopeless on the accordion with me?' In a flash his amazement turns to fury. He slaps me twice, and to help calm his mood, he snatches my favourite scores and tears them into little pieces.

One day my father rings the bell three times to summon me to the verandah. 'You'll soon be seven, so you can understand what I'm about to explain,' he says. 'I have already told you about German concentration camps during the war. When you arrive at a camp, everything you have is taken from you. If you have a gold tooth, they pull it out. Whether you're rich and beautiful or poor and ugly when you arrive, they put you in the same pyjamas and shave your head. Whatever skills you have, no one can see them. The guards are stupid and cruel. Showing signs of intelligence is dangerous.

'The only people who make it out of concentration camps alive are musicians. There have always been bands and there always will be. Because sheep would rather move about than think. The guards, who are the stupidest sort of sheep, love moving in time to music, and that's why they take care of the musicians and feed them better than the others.

'You need to know every type of music, but you'll have a better chance of getting out alive with a musette-waltz than a concerto. As for instruments, it's hard to predict which will be most in demand. So you'll study several. We're going to change your schedule so you have extra time to practise. I've asked Yves to give me a list of instruments to order for you. Off you go.'

Not for a second does my father take into consideration Yves's brutality; what matters above all else is his mastery of several instruments. Yves becomes my regular music teacher for many years to come. Spurred on by his insults and slaps, I learn to play guitar, clarinet, violin, tenor saxophone and trumpet, as well as piano and accordion. By the time I'm eight, I'll be pretty much equipped to survive in a concentration camp.

We Sagittarians

In his study my father has two safes, both bigger than I am. They are so huge and solid I find them almost beautiful, almost reassuring. One has a combination lock. My father sometimes summons me to this room to teach me how to open a safe without knowing the code. It will be very useful, he explains, if I am ever short of money. In the event that I am, I have to identify a casino to rob. The advantage of casino safes is that, even though they are full of money, they are not as closely guarded as those at the Banque de France. Once the safe is open, I must respect the rules: take only cash and leave jewellery and other valuables. It is when you come to trade in jewellery that you get caught, because the dealers are often in cahoots with the police.

He makes me sit on the floor and put my ear to the lock mechanism. While he carefully turns the graduated dials one way and then the other, I have to listen attentively to the sounds produced by the cogs turning on their axes. In a half-whisper he calmly describes each stage with a remarkable patience completely at odds with his usual brusque manner. I like these sessions when, deep in silence, we both strain our ears to pick up the barely perceptible *click-click-click-click* of the workings on the other side of that metal door.

The training never lasts very long. 'Right, it's time you went back to your schoolwork,' he says. Before leaving, I try to think of something nice to say to him. One time I ask, 'Do you think one day I'll be able to open safes like you?' 'You're my daughter,' he replies, 'you'll be able to open any safe.' Coming from him this is a genuine compliment and it warms my heart. I so want him to appreciate me a little!

Some days my father calls me into the large billiard room to teach me about the world with the help of a huge floor globe mounted on a stand and ringed by a wooden hoop. It is a beautiful thing and it fuels my dreams. I do not know what it is made of, but the surface is smooth and soft to the touch. When I'm alone in this room I stroke the planet Earth covered with magical places. I close my eyes and spin it, bringing a finger down at random, then open my eyes and whisper a promise to myself: 'You'll go there one day.' I contemplate the signs of the Zodiac engraved on the hoop. My father has taught me to recognize the centaur drawing back its bow. 'That's us,' he says, 'we Sagittarians.' He does not believe in 'astrological claptrap', but still has a soft spot for our sign. Whenever I can, I come to look at that fabulous creature, half-man, half-horse. I admire its strength, the bow drawn back and that arrow 'pointing in the right direction', as my father says, and he always adds a comment that I struggle to make sense of in relation to the arrow: 'Act wisely!'

One day I ask him what sign my mother is. He points a contemptuous finger at the poor scorpion, a shameful crawling creature. I feel bad for my mother. But I think that, as she is the sign just before ours, she must have some horse in her too.

Using the globe, my father shows me all the countries he flew over in a hot air balloon with his favourite copilot, my aunt Henriette. My father talks about her as if she were something extraordinary, an aviator like him and passionate about ballooning. I have met my aunt Henriette only once: shortly after we moved to the house she came over accompanied by two gorgeous collie dogs. I was too young to have anything more than vague memories of her.

Before the war, when my mother was a tiny baby, Henriette and my father often flew together and won ballooning races. He remembers with amusement all the times when, just before landing, he quickly had to throw off some ballast because Henriette had caught sight of a bull in the vicinity and refused point blank to touch down! And back up they would go, not knowing where or when they would be able to land again.

On one occasion a navigational error brought them over the German town of Landsberg an der Warthe during one of Hitler's speeches. My father shows me a photo of them with four German officers and two men in civilian clothes, my aunt smiling nervously in the middle of the group of men, who seem fascinated by this little slip of a woman wearing a man's checked shirt and riding breeches.

Henriette's thrills and spills always make my father laugh.

Listening to him, I start to think Henriette must be a really great person. If my mother and I can be just a fraction of who she is, we too might earn my father's indulgence and admiration.

During the war Henriette enlisted as a nurse and it was in a military hospital that she met the doctor who would become her husband. Meanwhile my father joined the Resistance in Lille. He dug underground passages to help Jews flee to Belgium. He also traded on the black market to make enough money to pay for food, residency papers and people smugglers for the fugitives.

My father's face lights up and his voice softens when he tells me about his younger days. I am fascinated not only by the stories he tells me, but by the expressions that suddenly brighten his usually deadpan features. He was a hero in his time. If only I had been born sooner, I could have met the passionate, dashing man he once was. The winged centaur crossing Europe on a misread compass needle. The Robin Hood risking his life to snatch the oppressed from the clutches of the Nazis. The great Freemason dignitary who 'did as he pleased', appearing, for example, before the Queen of England in red shoes. The 'charitable Knight of the Holy City' secretly working for the good of mankind. I still recall my amazement at this knight in full regalia, carrying his sword and with a large cross on his chest, as he appeared in my bedroom some evenings. But that was before. Before he decided to leave this abominable world and shut himself away with us in the house.

The last time my father ordered me to go to the workshop behind the swimming pool with him, he told me to unwrap a parcel: yards and yards of strange pale-yellow fabric. This special material was used for making balloons. It was from the post-war days when my father was working hard to relaunch hot air balloons at Bondues airfield. He and Henriette were the first to fly again, using airships they had made with their own hands. Sometimes I sneak off to touch that magic fabric, and I picture myself making a balloon so I can fly away with Linda and Pitou.

The Swimming Pool

Since I stopped having piano lessons with Madame Descombes, we hardly ever leave the house. Everything is arranged to keep outings to a minimum. There's no need to go to the bakery: we have a kneading trough and a professional oven in which my mother and I make bread twice a month. No need to go to the grocery store either: four times a year we ring though a large order on the telephone, and the goods are delivered by truck.

Every now and then, though, we do go out, always together and always in the Peugeot, which otherwise sits in the garage adjacent to the house. These outings are never simple operations, and we are all on edge. The car battery is often flat. It has to be recharged, which is enough to postpone plans or even cancel them. If by some stroke of luck the engine does start, everything has to happen very quickly: I'm already sitting in the front seat and my father has already started pulling out by the time my mother opens the gate; then she quickly swings it shut and hops into the back seat. The big Peugeot races off as if we have some vital mission to accomplish. In actual fact we're probably going to the market in Hazebrouck to buy chicks for the farmyard.

During the trip, I make myself as small as possible on the passenger seat. On these rare occasions when we do go out, my father always tells me to sit in the front. I can see my mother fuming at me in the rear-view mirror. Does she know I'd willingly swap places with her? 'You know that's the death seat,' she hisses when she and I are alone, out of my father's earshot. 'If he has to brake sharply, you'll go straight through the windscreen. If there's an accident, he'll die and take you along with him. That's why your father puts you there. But he's protecting me.'

I don't know why she resents me, and I don't comment. In any event, my mind is too full of the crippling tension that accompanies all our outings. My parents are even more painstaking than usual about keeping a close watch on me. I feel suffocated. Out of the corner of my eye, I snatch glimpses of so many things I'd love to go and look at, but my father sets us a return time that is down to the exact minute. He waits in the car and we do our shopping at breakneck speed with one eye on the clock.

Our last outing was three months ago now: to Hazebrouck to get a new stock of chicks. On the way back, my father stopped on the main square, and my mother and I nipped into the bookshop. I asked whether I could look at some books. 'Children's books are right there,' the bookseller said kindly.

'Hurry up, your father's waiting.' I took a book at random from the Pink Library Collection and another from the Green

Library Collection. My mother paid for them hastily and then hid them in her bag. She didn't have to tell me to keep quiet. My father wants me to read important books. He would definitely have forbidden me from reading this sort of thing, and would have crucified my mother for letting me have them. I was in turmoil all the way back. What if she refused to give them to me when we got home?

But on that particular day, a miracle happened. As soon as we were alone together, my mother handed me the package from the bookshop without a word. I went and hid the books between my mattress and my bedsprings. That evening I waited till there was no more noise coming from the other rooms and then examined my new treasures, the cardboard binding, the colour picture on the glossy front cover. It was the first time I'd read children's books. I'd picked them up thinking they were stories about two different libraries. In fact, one was from *The Famous Five* series, and the other was a Nancy Drew mystery.

Every evening after my day of lessons, music and manual labour, I'm allowed to read for half an hour in bed. When I'm sure my father's asleep, I make the most of my mother's rare act of indulgence and ecstatically plunge into the adventures of my child heroes. In awe, I read them over and over again. Nancy Drew and the Famous Five are my only escape. They open a window onto the dizzying world of life that my father won't let me explore.

One day my mother hears me humming a tune I'm learning on the piano, which is enough to send her into a fury. She remembers the two books and tells me to bring them to her. 'Your behaviour's been getting worse for a while now. It must be because of these books I was stupid enough to buy you. They're confiscated.' I look miserable, like every other time she scolds me. But it doesn't really matter much. I know my heroes' stories so well I can dive straight back into them in my imagination.

Occasionally my mother turns a blind eye to my breaches of discipline. Mostly, though, she's even stricter than my father. When he's around I can tell she's extremely nervous. What she dreads more than anything is looking like a bad, weak or incompetent teacher. Whenever she and I are alone in our classroom on the second floor, she pressures me to get 'better than excellent' academic results.

One of the first things she had to teach me was how to read and write. I remember how exasperated she was by my slow progress. I made mistakes when my father asked me to read a page out loud. I could see her out of the corner of my eye, her face darkening with shame and anger. Writing was even worse. Why did I have to learn to write with a quill and an inkwell? She oversaw every upstroke and downstroke of my letters, and flew into a rage at the tiniest smudge. She would tear the page out and give me another one to write on. I was still so young; I didn't know how to stop the tears from flowing. The ink on the page would soon be soaked, which made her even more hysterical. My hands were completely black by the end of those writing lessons.

My mother thinks of me as a shifty creature, a bottomless pit of ill will. Just as I clearly spatter ink on my pages deliberately, I also deliberately chip the glass top on the big dining-room table. I deliberately miss a step or tear the skin on my hands when I'm weeding the grounds. Or fall, or scratch myself. I'm a 'cheat' and

41

a 'faker'. I'm always trying to draw attention to myself.

While I was learning to read and write, I also learned to ride a bike. I had a child's bike with training wheels at the back. 'We're taking those off now,' my mother told me one day. My father was behind us, watching the scene in silence. My mother made me get onto my suddenly unstable bicycle, took hold of me with both hands and—*whoosh*—launched me down the sloping driveway. When I fell, I scraped my leg on the gravel. I burst into tears of pain and humiliation. But when I saw those two impassive faces watching me, my sobbing stopped. Without a word, my mother put me back on the bike and kept launching me as many times as it took for me to learn to balance on my own.

My scrapes were treated on the spot, my mother holding my knee firmly while my father poured surgical spirit straight onto my smarting wounds. Crying and moaning were forbidden. I had to 'grit my teeth'.

I learned to swim the same way. Of course, going to the local swimming pool was out of the question. The summer I was four, my father had a pool built 'especially for me' at the end of the garden. It was not a pretty pool with blue water, but rather a long thin strip enclosed by concrete walls. The water was dark and freezing cold, and I couldn't see the bottom.

As with the bike, my first lesson was simple and quick: my mother threw me into the water. I struggled and screamed and swallowed a lot of water. Just as I was about to plummet to the bottom, she dived in and fished me back out. And we started again. I wailed once more and cried and choked. My mother dragged me out again. 'You'll be punished for that stupid snivelling,' she said before pushing me unceremoniously back into the pool. My body struggled to avoid drowning while my spirit coiled up a little tighter inside me with every dunk.

'A strong person doesn't cry,' my father insisted, as he watched the performance out of range of the splashing. 'You need to know how to swim. It's vital in case you fall from a bridge or if you need to escape.' I gradually learned how to keep my head above water. And over time I've even become a good swimmer, but I hate the water, just as I hate that pool where I still have to train.

To show I'm not 'chicken', I now have to jump straight into the icy water without any fuss. It knocks the breath out of me every time. But my father insists I not miss a single opportunity to 'strengthen my powers of endurance'.

Cap Gris Nez

Some friends of my father's, a couple, Ginette and François, have come to spend a few days with us. I really like François; he is a small friendly man, almost completely bald and always even-tempered. He talks to me kindly, is funny and loves to laugh. There are plans for a rare outing: we are going to Cap Gris Nez, a cape that looks across to the English coast. 'Oh, it's going to be such fun!' says François, and I find his enthusiasm contagious. With him along, I am sure it will be much more enjoyable than an outing to the Hazebrouck market. The decision was made so easily. Maybe there will be other outings now. I feel as light as a butterfly.

But as soon as we reach the coast my father gives me a new exercise to 'toughen me up': he insists I go and lean over the cliff edge. No, no, no, I don't want to, I can't! I am now quite good at hiding my fear, but this time it's just impossible. I am so paralyzed with terror I cannot take a single step. Exasperated, my father gets my mother and Ginette to help catch me. They forcibly drag me to the lip of the precipice and hold me there with my head hanging over the edge. I contort in horror. With my eyes tight shut, I can feel the drop sucking me downwards. I feel sick with vertigo.

While I struggle, I catch sight of François's blue sweater and light-coloured pants a little way off. He pretends to be gazing at the scenery. He has his hands in his pockets and looks uncomfortable. I'm grateful to him for staying away from these grappling hands, against which I am completely powerless. I belong to my parents; I am their thing. There is no space for life inside me or around me. Do I scream? Do I sob? All I know is that they throw me into the back of the car and lock it.

And I, who dream of nothing more than getting out, now hope with all my might that I will be left locked in there…if the very thought of standing close to a cliff edge puts me into such a hysterical state then I must be too stupid, too cowardly and too much of a disappointment. My mother is right; if it weren't for them I would be in Bailleul.

The next day my father rings the bell three times. I'm being summoned. My heart starts racing. I immediately stop reading and go to look at the board in the pantry to see where the ringing is coming from: his bedroom. I climb the stairs full of foreboding, knock on the door and wait for his permission to go in. Then I sit down, careful to adopt the 'concentration position': neither too far forward nor too far back. My parents think that anyone who sits against the back of a chair is lazy, and those who sit on the edge are weak. My father runs his closed fist down my spine to check I'm not touching the back of the chair. Then he gives one of the front chair legs a sharp kick. If I'm too close to the edge I'll fall. Because I'm sitting 'correctly in the middle', this doesn't unbalance me.

Now he sits facing me and peers right into my eyes. Whatever happens, I mustn't look away.

He starts his 'teaching': 'The Third Reich was one of the strongest nations, better even than the Spartans. The nation of the Third Reich will return and it will rule the world. It is superior to all others because of the teaching and training it gives its youth. This education is *hard.*' He singles out the word without raising his voice. 'There is *no room for weakness.*' He articulates each word individually. 'Hard, cruel, strong young people with no fears, unshakeable. That is my lesson. No room for weakness. You need hard physical exercises. Your mind will triumph because it is stronger than your body, and then it will be able to control matter.'

He falls silent, his eyes still boring into mine. 'Now go,' he orders harshly after a while.

I stand up, making sure I don't scrape the chair on the floor. Scraping a chair after a teaching is forbidden.

My unspeakable behaviour at Cap Gris Nez warrants the maximum punishment: except for these teachings, I won't be spoken to for three weeks. Ginette and François won't speak to me either. Then, in the following three weeks, I will be spoken to only formally, and with no eye contact. Meanwhile, I myself won't be allowed to speak for the whole six-week period, except to answer questions, and I too must use the formal form of address and make no eye contact.

Even under normal circumstances, we talk very little. My father makes no conversation. He gives his 'teachings' or issues orders. Whenever he opens his mouth I listen, desperately attentive. I often find I don't understand a word he's saying, and start to panic inside. I force myself to keep my eyes on his, but I can feel my mind battering against the confines of my brain like a terrified bird. If I ever find the courage to ask a question during a meal, he roars, 'Only speak if you have something intelligent to say.' I don't understand the concept of 'intelligent', so mostly I stay silent. My mother talks about me, though, starting her sentences with 'she'. Sometimes my name is mentioned and I try to make myself as small as possible, even if what she's saying isn't negative, such as: 'Maude studied the second declension in Latin this morning.' It feels really strange. There are only two situations when I hear her say my name: when she's talking about me to my father and when she's yelling at me.

It turns out that being banned from speaking is far more horrible than I thought. I feel I've been imprisoned in a fortress of silence and it's growing smaller by the day; I'm no longer allowed to resist, no longer allowed to feel. It's like I'm disappearing inside myself. The hardest thing is mealtimes. We eat in a deathly hush. I'm so tense it makes me even clumsier: I spill my drink, I clink my cutlery on my plate. My father scowls at me furiously. I find it hard to swallow so I chew endlessly. 'Only the weak chew for a long time. Swallowing big pieces forces your stomach to work for you, and that builds your character and your strength.' When he was young he always succeeded in his own personal challenge of downing six hard-boiled eggs in the time it took the clock to strike twelve midday. But as hard as I try, I can't manage to swallow. 'That's enough now,' my mother screams eventually. 'Get out! Go and study!'

If I'm not on the brink of suicide, then it's thanks to a glorious consolation I've found to counter the emptiness of this silence: the conversations of animals. Whether I'm hunched over my homework or busy with manual labour, I secretly lend an ear to the constant chatter of birds in the garden. One asks a question, another replies, a third intervenes, then they all chat together. Occasionally a dog calls out in the distance…and then suddenly all the dogs in and around the village join in the general hubbub.

I try to work out what these heated discussions mean; they start with a private chat, quiet mutterings and every now and then burst into an intense, exuberant racket with all the animals talking at once. Is there a barnyard somewhere keenly greeting a newcomer? Or a stable block celebrating a mare being reunited with her foal? I think of Linda behind her bars. I'm sure she's listening intently too. But try as I might to strain my ears, I don't hear her voice in the chorus of dogs. Like me, has she been instructed not to speak?

When studying Bach's *Two- and Three-part Inventions* on the piano, I make an even more exciting discovery: music has conversations of its own. The right hand starts with a phrase, the left responds, the right picks it up again, the left follows. And, as with the animals, the two hands end up playing together. I'm thrilled by these dialogues. I play them over and over, never tiring of them. I gradually add my own improvisations based on the cheeping I can hear from the garden: my right hand reproduces a phrase from a bird's melody, and my left does a pastiche of another bird's response. I reproduce their exchange as faithfully as I can, then let my hands run freely over the keyboard, simulating someone dutifully following the score. To disguise my ploy, I pretend to be working on a piece my parents don't know. They can't read music so they're completely taken in.

Several months after these periods of silence, I still find it hard to get sounds out of my mouth. I stammer and blush, I scramble my words. The worst thing is when, on the way downstairs, my mother warns me quietly, 'You'd better not make any mistakes, Monsieur Didier is going to test you.' I'm shaking by the time I get to him. He ends each of his questions with 'Think carefully before you reply.' That's all it takes for my voice to start quavering and descend into pathetic stuttering. When he yells 'Enunciate when you speak! E-nun-ci-ate!', all that comes out of my throat is a husky gurgling. Infuriated, my father sends me away: 'Leave! Come back when you know.' I withdraw, fighting back my tears. I know the answers; I just can't get them out.

My parents are convinced I stammer on purpose, to disguise the fact that I haven't learned my lessons. They are both very annoyed. My mother is frightened she will be held responsible for my poor performance. My father, on the other hand, shudders to think that—despite all his efforts and all the training he puts me through—I'm proving in the long run to be what he hates most in the world: a 'wet blanket'.

'You listen to me,' he always says, 'we're not like everyone else. We're not sheep. We belong to the category of strong spirits. You will develop a strong mind like mine. Don't disappoint me, don't grow into a weakling like your mother.' Bending over me from his giant's height, he says this without taking his eyes off me, emphasizing each syllable, terrifying as an Olympian god. Ever since I've learned about Greek mythology, I can see Zeus, the god of thunder and lightning, in my father's features.

The Cellar

It's the middle of the night. The three of us are going down the stairs into the cellar. I'm wearing a sweater over my pyjamas, but I'm barefoot. I'm not usually allowed to walk about barefoot in case I catch cold. I shiver as I climb down the stairs, afraid of hurting myself on something sharp. In front of me is my father's imposing silhouette. Behind me, my mother, locking the door. Why is she locking it? I don't understand what's going on and start shaking. With every step we go a little deeper into the odour of the cellar, a stench of damp and mould that turns my stomach.

My father sits me on a chair positioned in the middle of the largest room. I can hear his heavy breathing and I can see the bristly grey stubble that has grown since he shaved yesterday morning. I look around surreptitiously to see whether there are any mice. The coal heap isn't far away, and there may be rats hiding behind it. I nearly faint at the thought.

'You're going to stay here without moving,' my father says. 'You're going to meditate on death. Open up your brain.' I have no idea what that means, but I don't even try to understand. What more will he demand of me? What will happen to me? They're not going to leave me here, are they? And my worst fear is realized: I hear them walking away behind me, and then the cellar light goes out. There's still a faint glow coming from the stairs. Then, suddenly, darkness.

They've left, and turned off the lights.

My eyes frantically probe the darkness. Only my ears can make anything out, and what they hear propels me into an abyss of terror. A host of sinister noises, little animals moving around in the dark, scurrying, running, stopping, rummaging and scuttling off again. I'm screaming inside, but no sound comes out because my lips are clamped shut and quivering. My father told me that if I open my mouth, mice or even rats will sense it and will climb up me, get into my mouth and eat me from the inside. He's seen several people die like that in cellars when he was taking shelter from air raids in World War I. I worry that the mice might be able to get in through my ears. But if I cover them with my hands I won't hear anything, I'll be blind and deaf.

I'm a pathetic puddle of fear. I move and breathe as little as possible, I stifle my shaking and chew the insides of my cheeks to stop my teeth from chattering, I try to disappear, make myself transparent, nonexistent. Maybe the rodents will forget I'm here. But I'm sick to my stomach. I'm afraid that my bladder's going to give way; that is bound to be the sort of smell to immediately attract a whole family of rats. I can hear their busy little feet around me. Sometimes their pattering comes closer. Sometimes I hear one of them stop and feel a leg of my chair. It makes my insides liquefy. My feet fly off the ground reflexively. I hold them up, but it's painful. Every now and then I have to lower them. I do it infinitely carefully, to avoid putting them down directly onto some rodent's back or teeth.

At last the light comes back on; my mother has come to get me. I don't so much walk as fly towards the stairs and practically go up them on all fours, as fast as I can, towards that open door that I simply must reach before it closes again. I know there's no reason why it should close now. But a voice inside me is screaming, 'Hurry up, get out quick, or you'll be locked in here forever.' I can hear my mother behind me: 'Look at this chicken!' I couldn't care less. I have to get out.

I went to such a faraway place inside my head that night, fear was so deeply imprinted on my body, that I don't remember feeling relieved when it ended. I don't recall the rest of the night, how I slept, or what state I was in when I woke. The next day was the same as usual. There was no compensation for the hours of sleep missed or the emotional torture during my test. 'Otherwise, how would it be a test?' my father said.

A month later, my parents wake me in the middle of the night again, and I know in a flash: it wasn't a one-off test, it was the first in a series of monthly training sessions they're going to inflict on me. I don't know how I manage to put one foot in front of the other. I go down those stairs like an automaton, not even trying to escape. As if I'm chained to a conveyor belt trundling me towards a cleaver which will slice me up. I'm soon overwhelmed by the nauseating smell of the cellar. I'm suffocating all over again in the horror of absolute darkness and silence. I pray with all my might for it to end, for me to disappear. I ask for death, I beg it to come and take me. Is that what 'meditating on death' means?

One night, when the three of us are going down the cellar stairs, my very tall father forgets to bend down and smacks his forehead violently into a metal beam. The test is immediately aborted. When my father is injured or sick everything stops straightaway until he has recovered. So we hurry back upstairs to tend to his wound. I'm secretly relieved, but I also feel guilty. I'm a bad daughter to be delighting in my father's injury. A bad daughter who will have to pay for her bad thoughts.

I don't have to wait very long. The following month my father doesn't come with me when I go down to the cellar. On my way down, I notice that a piece of yellow foam has been secured to the place where he hit his head last time. In a flash of nostalgia, I remember the unexpected happiness I felt then. So I really am a bad person. And here's my punishment: before making me sit on a stool, my mother makes me put on a vest with little bells stitched onto it. I no longer have the option of leaning against a backrest, which means I no longer have the option of holding my feet up. If I move, my parents will hear the little bells ring. I decide it doesn't matter, nothing matters anymore.

But I can feel my heart accelerate in direct proportion to how far up the stairs my mother has climbed. The light goes out; I hear the key turn in the lock. Once again, darkness engulfs me. Once again, I'm a slave to those sounds. I have shoes on this time. Every now and then I clack them together, taking great care not to let the bells on my vest ring. It must work because just after I've smacked my shoes together, I hear little paws scurrying away.

*

My father tells me why I need to meditate on death: it's so that I get used to the kingdom of the dead, so I feel at ease with the dead and they with me. Darkness allows us to communicate with them. Later I'll have to travel between the kingdom of the living and the kingdom of the dead. I don't think he knows it's not the dead I'm terrified of, but the rats. I don't say anything because I'm convinced that, if he knew, he'd think of some horrible way to cure me of my fear.

Arthur

After learning to ride a bike and to swim, I now have to learn to ride a horse. My father insists I be as accomplished a horsewoman as Will Scarlet's Maude. He also has more practical motives. First, just like swimming, riding will be very useful if I need to escape. Secondly, it will be a prerequisite when, like my father, I'm initiated into a chivalric order—passing myself off as a man, it goes without saying. However much I turn this idea over in my mind, I still find it puzzling. Yes, my father is a knight, but he has never ridden a horse…

There is a third and still more indisputable reason: I need to be able to get a job with a circus in case I have to hide or go undercover at some point. No one asks for your papers in a circus, they ask you to ride well, to walk on your hands and do somersaults. 'You're going to learn all of these skills,' my father tells me. 'We're starting with horseback riding.'

Of course, there's no question of my joining a riding club. I'll learn under my mother's instruction on the estate, where there is already a small stable near the duck pond. My father has just bought a horse from a man in the village. He's a darling piebald pony named Arthur. For Arthur and me, it's love at first sight. When he sees me, his eyes light up. He nudges me, then drops his head so I can get onto his back. I climb up his neck by holding on to his mane, and end up facing the wrong way. He waits for me to turn around, and then off we go along the pathways on the grounds.

I ride him bareback, grasping his mane in my hands. I couldn't be happier. I love the way Arthur smells; I love the sound of his hooves clopping on the red gravel. When we get to the lawn he goes faster, but not too fast: he is careful not to make me fall. I bounce on his back in time to his little trot, and my heart leaps for joy.

Sometime later a package arrives in the mail: a glossy brown saddle that gives off a strong smell of leather and cost 20,000 francs. My parents keep reminding me how expensive it was. All I can think is that it's a bit heavy for a pint-sized mount like Arthur. My mother wants to show me how to tack up. She slips on a bridle, then puts the saddle on his back and starts fastening the girth, without realizing that Arthur is puffing out his stomach. Next she puts one foot in the stirrup and pushes herself off the ground to swing her other leg over his hindquarters. That's when the cheeky pony quickly sucks in his stomach, which makes the saddle slip and...*Crash!* Now she is sprawled on the ground between Arthur's legs, looking very put out. Her hair has come undone and there are bobby pins scattered all over the gravel. Meanwhile, Arthur is looking very regal, holding his head high as if the episode doesn't warrant any attention at all.

My mother gets to her feet and kicks Arthur in the stomach. His unshakeable composure, his refusal to be annoyed, to rear up or bite, makes me throw my head back and laugh uncontrollably. She storms off, leaving us to it. Even the slap she gives me on her way past only makes me laugh harder. I'm hiccupping by the time I release the girth and take off the saddle, which is so heavy I stumble under its weight. Then I undo the noseband and take out the bit. My father watches this scene without a word. I can feel his disapproving eyes on my back, but I try not to think about it—I might burst out laughing again.

Two weeks later a whip arrives in another parcel. My mother saddles up Arthur again. But this time a few cracks of the whip persuade him to hold in his stomach, so she manages to tighten the girth properly and mount him. Arthur sets off, but at a slow walk, his head held low, refusing to break into a trot. 'Watch closely,' my mother says. 'This is how to ride, not the way you do, like a little feral child.' I don't know exactly what 'feral' means, but it sounds quite nice. I'm happy to be feral, especially if it includes all the fun Arthur and I have together.

Arthur has another love: Linda. At various times during the day I see him standing right outside her metal gate. When I have to shut her in at ten to eight in the morning, Arthur tries to get into the kennel too. It's impossible, of course. But I know they catch up with each other during the night: Linda goes to join him in his stable. Before I go to sleep I picture them curled up together. I imagine myself snuggled in their warmth.

Can an animal teach a person about happiness? In the depth of my despair, I am fortunate to have this incredible source of joy. My heart swells with affection at the thought of spending time with Arthur. Or just the thought of walking past him, of catching the adoring look he gives me as I pass. At night I remember the way he looked, unperturbed, patiently taking those kicks. And I laugh quietly under the covers. I love Arthur. I love Linda. Linda loves Arthur, Arthur loves Linda. Together we're strong and beautiful, even if things are difficult. If only for our fleeting moments of love, everything else is worth putting up with.

And there's more and more to bear. 'Tough pedagogy' means I have to get used to Spartan living conditions. Of course, all distractions must be eliminated. I have to learn to sleep as little as possible, because sleep is a waste of time. I also have to cope without any of life's pleasures, starting with delights for the tastebuds, which are the surest route to weakness. My mother arranges for butter, flour, sugar, oil, yeast, et cetera to be delivered in bulk. But we are never allowed fruit, yoghurt, chocolate, or any other kind of treat. For the sake of my training, I also have to respect special rules, like never eating fresh bread. My portion of the bread we bake every two weeks is systematically set aside to go stale.

Indulging oneself is a serious sin. My father is determined to take the magic out of any kind of celebration, particularly the holiday season, the worst of all, with all the forced cheerfulness it creates around the world. I have to train myself not to fall for these misguided celebrations. For us, Christmas and New Year's mean an increased workload. After dinner my mother and I have to go back up to the classroom and study for six more hours, until two in the morning. And the curriculum consists of the most daunting subjects like Latin, German and maths…The next day, despite my missing hours of sleep, my father won't allow any changes to the usual schedule.

At Christmas last year, the postman came and offered us some calendars being sold by the post office. My father invited him in and poured him a glass of cognac. Then he said, 'Go ahead, Maude, choose a calendar.' I studied them one at a time; they were all so beautiful! I eventually chose one with a picture of an adorable litter of puppies. When I looked up, I caught my father's eye; he was glowering at me furiously.

Eventually my mother slipped a banknote to the postman and showed him out. My father turned towards me. His voice boomed like a clap of thunder: 'When I tell you to choose, Maude, that doesn't mean "choose". It means take what's in front of you decisively so no one can detect the slightest hesitation on your part. Choosing has nothing to do with pleasure. Only the weak hesitate and take pleasure in choosing. Life isn't about pleasure, it's a merciless struggle. If you show someone what gives you pleasure, you're revealing your vulnerability, and that person will take advantage of them to crush you. When you behave the way you just have, you put us all in danger.'

I'm sure my father's right. But still, how can he accuse me of being obsessed with pleasure? I know what pleasure is, it's mentioned in books: ice-cream, cakes, parties, dances, Christmas trees…These are all things I've never seen or experienced, and to be honest I don't miss them. My father need not worry, I've never dreamed of or longed for a Christmas tree.

What I do dream of are butterflies and beetles and clover leaves. Snapdragons that look like little mouths when you pinch them open, and I imagine I'm chatting to them, regretting that I'm not a ventriloquist to give them words to match their moving lips. Gooseberries that Arthur and I pick in secret to feast on their bitter taste. Birds flying in the sky, unhindered by the fences of the house. And turtledoves, especially when they smooch with each other.

Since the incident with the calendar, I've grasped that I have to disguise my delight and enthusiasm for things. Now, when I see something wonderful, I act completely indifferent to it.

The Killer

In my father's view, comfort is one of the pernicious 'pleasures' that must be suppressed. Beds must not be cosy, sheets must not be soft to the touch, nor chairs relaxing. Given the long hours I spend at the piano, Madame Descombes had suggested many times that my stool be swapped for a Beethoven chair with a backrest. To no avail, of course.

By the same token, despite the icy winters in the north of France, the vast house is barely heated. My bedroom must not be heated at all in order to conform to the precepts of a 'tough' upbringing. Sometimes it's so cold that my windows freeze over on the inside. For half the year, going to bed and getting up in the morning are torture, so I try to undress and dress as fast as I can.

For the same reasons, I have to wash in cold water. 'Hot water is for wimps. If you're ever in prison later in life, you need to show that you're not afraid of ice-cold water. You should even be able to wash using snow, and without a second thought.' My parents, on the other hand, are allowed hot water, especially my father, who—because he's 'the very picture of strong will'—has nothing left to prove.

We bathe once a week. My father doesn't believe in the virtues of daily bathing: 'Your body secretes a layer of antibodies to protect you from germs. When you take a bath, you lose your immunity and expose yourself to diseases,' he tells me, and then adds, 'unless you bathe in the same water as me: I protect you from outside pollutants.' That's why I have to wait until my parents have taken their baths before I can get into the tub, without changing the water. 'Leaving my water for you is an honour I grant you,' my father often says. 'It allows you to benefit from my energies when they enter your body.' Not only has the water had more than enough time to cool, but it's covered in a nasty grey scum mixed in with the Lux soap flakes. I wash in haste, keeping my eyes and mouth tightly shut, trying to breathe as little as possible.

In the interest of 'toughening me up', I now have to join my mother and watch the butcher, who comes every four or five months to slaughter animals that my father has had delivered to the house. The butchering lasts two or three exhausting days, each starting with a 3:30 a.m. wake-up call. The man we call 'The Killer', an employee at the slaughterhouse in Wormhout, arrives at four o'clock in the morning. While we wait for the delivery truck, we give him a glass of white wine in the kitchen. He makes such stupid conversation that my mother and I exchange looks of wide-eyed amazement. I stare, fascinated, at his one remaining tooth, a brown stump dangling from his upper jaw, which he constantly wiggles with his tongue.

I have to go with him when he takes the animal from the truck. If it's a steer, we go into the stables. He takes a kind of punch pistol from his bag and puts it between the animal's eyes. And shoots. The steer falls to the ground instantly with a dull thud. He hangs it head-down on a hook. If it's a sheep or a pig, we take it outside, by the henhouse, and the Killer slits its throat with a big knife. Then he drags the carcass into the stable to hang it up. It's harder with pigs. They understand what's in store and fight for their lives. Their screams make my blood run cold.

The Killer doesn't let that stop him. He carries on with his task as if he were chopping wood. He tells me the animals need to hang for twenty-four hours to ensure the meat's not tough. So off he goes and doesn't come back until the following morning, still just as early, this time to cut up the carcasses. First he cuts them into quarters and carries a quarter at a time down to the cellar, where we wait for the next step of the process. As he butchers the meat, my mother and I wrap up the cuts. The name of each joint has to be written on a label before it's put into the freezer. With a steer or a sheep there are hundreds of cuts, which gradually fill up the three freezers that stand side by side, connected to a generator. Then we get to the lesser cuts: the Killer empties out the intestines and makes blood pudding. We work through the evening, surrounded by the awful smell of blood and raw meat. Sometimes the job isn't finished and the Killer has to come back again the next day.

I loathe being shut up in that cellar, submerged in the smell of death. My back hurts and I feel sick. These packets of meat seem to go on forever. But the worst thing of all is when the Killer kills a veal calf. The calf has to stay calm and relaxed so its delicate meat doesn't 'spoil'. It's my job to spend time with it and soothe it. With his wide, toothless grin, the Killer says, 'Ah, there's nothing like a child and, even better, a little girl, to keep animals calm.'

So I'm left alone with the calf, which is chained up by the stables. How long do I have to stay there? I'm a little bit frightened of it, it's a lot bigger than me. I'm also frightened of failing in my mission. My father told me we'll know straightaway tomorrow, from the colour of the meat, whether I've done it properly. If the meat is pink, it's ruined; we'll have to bring in another calf to be killed. I talk to the animal softly and pray its meat won't be pink. But the more I stroke it, the more my heart goes out to it. I wish time could stand still, and its death could be postponed indefinitely.

I didn't hear him come over, but the Killer is suddenly standing in front of the animal and in one swift move, he puts the pistol to its forehead. The calf slumps to the ground. It seems to me that its eyes convey the helpless question: 'Why?' I sometimes fall too, my foot caught under the inanimate body. The Killer hauls me out, laughing uproariously.

During slaughtering time, I'm overwhelmed by lack of sleep, exhaustion, the stench, and the violence of my emotions. My mother's nerves are frayed too. From time to time, out of nowhere, we both succumb to convulsive laughter. If, for example, the Killer pulls a ridiculous face or makes some idiotic comment, we find it incredibly hard to regain our composure. We only have to catch each other's eye to shriek with laughter all over again.

At mealtimes we make superhuman efforts to repress our hilarity. My father finds laughter extremely irritating. He sees it as a waste of energy, proof of a total lack of control. Smiling finds no favour in his eyes either. 'Do you want to be the village idiot?' he asks if he catches me gazing up at the sky with a smile on my face. 'Only halfwits smile. Your face must be serious and expressionless in order to confuse your adversaries. Never reveal anything.'

We escape to the kitchen with the excuse that we're getting the dessert. Having a guest at the table is one of the rare times that a meal ends with apple tart, made with apples from the garden. Last time the Killer came, there was a mishap. On the way out to the verandah, the tart slipped and landed on a handful of Linda's hair! My mother and I looked at each other in horror, certain my father was going to rip us to shreds in front of this cretin. Without a word we picked up the tart and went back to the kitchen. My mother scraped it clean with a knife as best she could, before putting it back on the serving dish.

With his first mouthful the Killer almost choked. 'How strange,' he said between two coughing fits, 'it's like I've swallowed a hair.' While my father, serious as a judge, watched him splutter, my mother and I busied ourselves clearing the table, eyes lowered, making absolutely sure we didn't catch each other's eye. Then we hurried out to the kitchen where we could collapse laughing at last. Many long minutes later we'd calmed down enough to look at each other without exploding again. For a moment my mother's eyes, still intoxicated with mirth, looked into mine. Then, in a flash, we looked away, embarrassed. We weren't used to that.

Shoots and Roots

Life is made up of two sorts of people, just as there are two types of roots: those that set to work straightaway and bore into the ground wherever they are, not wasting any time, pursuing the task even if they hit pebbles or bricks, and inching slowly down; and those that want to drive into the earth as quickly as possible, and so opt to find the "right" soil first. Sometime later, the first type, the roots, have succeeded in delving deep into the earth while the second, the shoots are still drifting here and there, having failed to find a spot that offers no resistance.

I have to follow the example of those first roots, the ones that triumph with their perseverance. But the thought that someday I'll be completely buried in the ground terrifies me. I'd much rather be the sort that skips about but never settles. I don't say this, of course, but my parents seem to have guessed. When I take an interest in something that isn't a planned part of my schooling—asking to study Spanish or to learn to jump rope, for example—my father admonishes me severely with a 'shoots and roots!'

After reading *The Pied Piper of Hamelin*, I wanted to learn to play the pipe. Given how many instruments I have to play, I didn't think this would be a problem. It earned a 'Shoots and Roots!' If during a lesson I ask a question about the subject we're currently studying, like, say, 'How do Eskimo children live?' my mother replies, 'What did your father teach you about shoots and roots?'

Perhaps because of my secret preference for those flighty shoots, or my inappropriate curiosity, or what is surely an overly strong yearning to go and see the world beyond the fence, we have completely stopped going on outings and it's been months now since anyone has mentioned a trip to the market in Hazebrouck or anywhere else. When my father summons me, he keeps reiterating his parable of the roots. He must think me too much of a scatterbrain.

Sometimes he orders me to stare at the old clock on the mantelpiece in the dining room. 'Now you listen to me, Maude: you're going to watch that clock and not think about anything else, and you'll keep doing it until I tell you to stop.' My father so likes these glass-domed clocks with golden pendulums that he bought a whole batch of them. They have pride of place in at least seven or eight rooms in the house. Of course, he has no idea that I loathe them. I see them as enemies. I'm frightened of them, but at the same time I'm contemptuous of them, with their stupid mechanism, their fake gilding, their endless 'I swing this way, then I swing that way, nip to the left, nip to the right' and the ridiculous pride they take in living under glass…

On the way up to lessons this morning my mother announces out of the blue, 'As of this evening, you're changing bedrooms. You're seven now, you're old enough. Your father has decided.' I wonder why he's reached this decision. I suspect it's not so much to put me further away from my mother as to limit any opportunities for distraction. My room looks out over the street and, by an extraordinary stroke of luck, has no shutters. Has he realized that I slip my head under the red velvet curtain every evening and secretly watch the wonderful life of the people across the street? I observe them wandering casually from room to room, chatting, watching TV. Sometimes they open a tin of cookies and snack from it. I'm amazed to think you can eat like that, without being at the table, without asking permission. And this is with all the lights on, as if they had no idea about marksmen lying in wait.

I start shaking apprehensively as bedtime draws near. I don't know where I'll end up tonight. All the rooms frighten me. The one I'm least afraid of is the guest bedroom. It's intimidatingly big, but at least one of its windows opens onto the street, onto cars, passers-by, life. I desperately hope I'll be given that room.

In the evening my parents tell me to gather up my things. It doesn't take long, I have just one pair of pyjamas, a toothbrush, a thick cardigan, two pairs of socks and four pairs of underwear. I follow them along the landing. We walk past the guest bedroom. We go beyond the door to my father's vast room and stop at the next one. 'This is where you'll be from now on. So I can hear everything you do. Now close that shutter,' my father says. Before leaving, he explains that he has to lock my door, 'in case burglars break into the house, so they don't come and attack you.'

I'm left alone, unsettled by the strange smell of this unfamiliar room. I'm so sad and so cold, far from the glow of streetlights and sounds from outside. There's nothing now to come between me and my night-time terrors.

By changing bedrooms I've moved into a new phase of life. I now have to respect my schedule to the minute. Every morning we synchronize our watches, 'exactly as bombers and terrorists do', explains my father because, like them, our success depends on precision. My father, who is extremely punctual, gave me an adult's watch when I turned five and expected me to know how to tell the time.

Ever since I was little I've had to respect a tight schedule. Recently my mother has taken to timing my trips to the bathroom; as soon as I go beyond three minutes she comes knocking at the door. 'Is this going to take much longer? Come out right away!' Now it's the whole day—from the wake-up call at six o'clock to bedtime at eleven-thirty—that has to be regulated like clockwork. The day has to follow a detailed program devised by my parents and written out in a large exercise book, which I'm not allowed to read. My mother reads it to me, often in my father's presence.

If there are any changes, such as when my music teacher moves a lesson to the following day or there's some special project in the garden, she writes them in the book. I'm informed of these changes at mealtimes. Every day of my life is laid out in that book, from Monday morning to Sunday evening, summer and winter alike, with no exceptions. The time I wake up or go to bed can change if we have to assist the Killer, or during the 'holidays'. But even these variations obey immutable rules.

Another major change: I now have to take responsibility

for waking the household, which means I have to get up before everyone else. I do have an old alarm clock, but I'm not allowed to use it; I have to be able to wake by sheer force of will. Sometimes when the working day has gone on longer than usual, I secretly wind up the alarm clock and stuff it under my blankets in the hope of muffling its ringing. But it's a pointless precaution. I'm so terrified of being caught red-handed that I might as well have swallowed an alarm clock: my eyes snap open just before the appointed time. Every morning I breathe a sigh of relief to think I've avoided failure, humiliation and punishment.

The Schedule

Having woken at six, I have to be dressed and ready in ten minutes. I now have a key to unlock my door and go and wake my mother at six-ten precisely. My father emphasizes the point 'When I say six-ten, I don't mean six-oh-nine or six-eleven.' I wait in my room until the minute hand is on nine, then go and stand in the corridor. At the exact second the hand hits ten, I knock on her door.

Next I go downstairs to have my breakfast in the kitchen, in the space of ten minutes, standing so as not to waste time. I reheat the coffee that was prepared the day before, and pour some condensed milk into my drinking bowl. I don't like the smell of this milk but I have to drink it 'to build me up', like the two spoonfuls of sugar I have to add to the coffee. I take the piece of hardened bread that was deliberately left out for me the night before. From time to time I furtively dunk it in my coffee. I know this is strictly forbidden, but sometimes I have such bad toothaches that I risk violating this rule, all the while on the alert for footsteps.

Sometimes my mother comes downstairs without a sound and hides in the pantry to watch me. When I was little I would jump out of my skin at suddenly finding her standing motionless behind me. She would stare at me in silence, then give the beginnings of a wan smile as if to say, 'I'm watching you, you won't get away from me.' I wouldn't be able to swallow, feeling guilty of some terrible crime, but what exactly?

I now know the noises in the house so well that I can make out the tiniest sound. I can tell when she's tiptoeing downstairs, and when she's stationed herself behind the pantry door. I don't look around. I can hear she's holding her breath, and I too breathe as little as possible. I am exemplary: eating standing up, then rinsing out my bowl. Afterwards I hear her leave again, and this is soon confirmed by the creak of a particular stair.

At six-twenty I go to the dining room if it's winter, the verandah if it's summer, for half an hour of solfège. While I sol-fa aloud, I use a baton to beat out the time on a wooden box my father had made, so that my mother can monitor my work while she gets on with things in the kitchen.

At six-fifty I go into the garden for twenty minutes of brisk walking, with strict instructions to wear very few clothes. In winter it's very cold and completely dark. The light from the kitchen courtyard is my only bearing. With just a flashlight I have to head over to the aviary and the greenhouse, the part of the grounds that can't be seen from outside the estate. My father insists I never take the same route twice. 'As you do it every day, you must absolutely vary the circuit, otherwise someone who has climbed over the wall would know where to hide to kidnap you.'

I'm very cold but happy to be going to this part of the garden. Linda follows me in the dark, I can feel her behind me. I daren't talk to her for fear of attracting 'people lying in wait'. We go to see Arthur in the stable, I stroke him quietly and bury my face in his mane. The smell of him warms my frozen bones.

In springtime, when the mornings get lighter, I have to stop by the henhouse and collect the eggs. Sometimes I also have to go to the duck shed. I hate this. I know that muskrats hide in there overnight. With my stomach knotted in fear, I rummage through the straw looking for duck eggs. Sometimes it's beyond me, so I claim there weren't any eggs that day. Maybe the rats ate them?

Then I go up to the classroom alone for forty minutes to revise the work my mother will test me on during the day. At seven-fifty I go downstairs to find Linda and put her in her kennel. I have to do it quickly before the crucial event: waking my father. At precisely seven-fifty-eight I join my mother in her bedroom, and every day she says the same ritual sentence: 'Now go and wake Monsieur Didier and see if he's in a good mood.' We both know it has nothing to do with his mood. In fact, I have to go and check whether he's still alive, because every evening before going to bed my father announces with grim innuendo, 'I don't know whether I'll still be here in the morning.'

At eight o'clock I knock on my father's door with a shaking hand. For a few interminable seconds I worry that I've committed yet another terrible wrongdoing, that some awful disaster is about to unfold and it will be entirely my fault. Then at last I hear him call: 'Come in.' For the next forty minutes I wait on my father. I don't turn on the light straightaway so as not to hurt his eyes. I open the double drapes, switch on the small light in his bathroom and only then the lamp by his bed.

While he gets up and sits on the edge of the bed, I fetch the chamber pot. It's no ordinary pot, but a bowl made of glass so he can check for traces of white in his urine, a sign of excess albumen. I stand in front of him so he can urinate into the pot. Every morning I feel increasingly nauseous as the bowl gradually warms in my hands. I don't want to see, so I close my eyes, but I can't block my nose. I totter as I carry the pot away and empty it into the toilet on the same floor.

My mother comes into the bedroom with a tray. We prop up the pillows behind my father, who is sitting back up in bed, and we stand and watch as he drinks coffee with cream and eats buttered bread.

When he has finished, we dress him. He is sixty-two years old and not an invalid; he could do it himself. But he stands there passively, allowing us to handle him as we put on his pants and cardigan. I have the 'privilege' of putting on his socks and shoes.

While my father goes down to get comfortable in the dining room, my mother and I go up to the second floor. It is eight-forty and the morning lesson will go on for just over two hours, until eleven. Then I have to go back down for an hour of German with my father, during which my mother makes lunch.

I dread even more the lessons with my father than those with my mother. He doesn't really know German. His method consists of having me stand before him reciting sentences he has told me to learn by heart, without giving any indication of how to pronounce them. I also have to read out loud from works by

Schiller and Goethe or from the libretto of Mozart's *Magic Flute*. I make countless mistakes for which he roars at me and issues punishments.

At noon we sit at the table. Lunch lasts fifteen minutes.

From twelve-fifteen until my father goes to bed at 10 p.m., the time is divided into a precisely ordered sequence of duties: schoolwork, music, sports, tending the animals (hens, ducks, rabbits and budgerigars). There is just one break for supper, which lasts fifteen minutes and is taken at 8 p.m. just after I've let Linda out for the night.

At 10 p.m. my mother and I are back in my father's bedroom for half an hour for his bedtime routine. Then we each withdraw to our own bedroom. I'm allowed an hour to read, a so-called 'free' hour. The truth is I mostly read books chosen by my father. Lights out is at eleven-thirty. To be absolutely sure I'm sleeping, my mother is instructed to cut off the electricity supply to my bedroom.

The three of us comply with this schedule, which only changes to accommodate the major projects in the garden instigated by my father each summer. During these weeks when, as a lowly labourer, I have to learn the tough but noble craft of bricklaying, my classroom hours are replaced by manual labour.

I sleep for six and a half hours, and work or study for fifteen or sixteen hours. I'm often exhausted, while my mother carries out my father's instructions without tiring. I hate myself for this lack of endurance. I try to follow her example in the hope that one day I'll be as strong as she is.

The Hole

Every evening when we go up to bed, my father tells me to lock my door and stresses that I should leave the key in the lock. 'So that burglars can't get in by picking the lock,' he explains.

But there are times when he tells me *not* to leave the key in the lock. Then I know I'm likely to undergo a 'test of courage': the door to my room might burst open in the middle of the night and I will have to head off into the garden alone to learn how to exercise my bravery. Quite often, despite the instruction to take out the key, nothing happens. My father is keen on the element of surprise. I have to learn to confront every ordeal—whether scheduled or unexpected—with unshakeable resolve.

In fact, even though I have been warned, when my father's hand grips my doorhandle I sit up in bed with a terrible start. I then have thirty seconds—timed with a watch—to get dressed.

While my father goes back to his own room to stand by the window, I have to go out alone into the garden steeped in darkness. The test consists of walking around the grounds following a specific route: from the kitchen door to the workshop at the far end of the garden, via the duck pond and the swimming pool, then back through the bushes to the kitchen. At each staging point I have to switch on a light, count to three, then switch it off so my father can follow my progress from his post at the window.

I don't know whether he deliberately chooses moonless nights, but as soon as I get any distance from the house, the light from the courtyard, which is meant to give me my bearings, disappears completely. I walk deeper and deeper into a black hole. Even Linda doesn't have the courage to come with me. Numbed by the cold, I pick my way by feeling the tops of shrubs I can't see. I know I'm near the pond when I can make out the contour of the Australian poplar that I'm heading towards, sometimes with the help of the faint moonlight. Often, though, it's so dark that I can't see anything at all. Then, I know I have to walk twenty-eight paces to the right after the last shrub, in order to reach the poplar. My heart pounds in my chest while my hands reach for the fence around the ducks' enclosure. I can hear frightening rustles and hisses. At last I find the first light switch and turn it on.

During my slow count of three, I plot out the next stage. In the distance behind me I can make out my father's silhouette framed in the window, as he watches my journey, rifle in hand. Now I switch off the light and, still feeling my way using the bushes along my route, I head towards the rotunda, where the second light switch is located. Then on to the third light switch by the workshop. After that I have to complete the longest section,

78

which brings me back to the fence at the front of the house. I find my bearings by running my hand over the tops of bushes and keeping an eye on my father's lighted window.

But the window always goes dark halfway through the circuit, suddenly plunging me into total blackness. Does he do it on purpose? Is this yet another technique to strengthen my courage? Panic takes hold of me. The house is still too far away and I now have only the bushes to guide me. I lose all sense of direction and stray into the undergrowth. Behind me and all around me, I hear a host of disturbing noises, footsteps, rustling leaves. I'm so tense it's as if I have a giant cramp in my whole body.

It takes a tremendous effort to keep calm, to put one foot in front of the other until I see the weak light from the courtyard. The circuit ends with me climbing back upstairs exhausted and freezing. It's one of the few occasions when I get back to my room with something like relief, almost a feeling of safety, tainted with a strange sadness. I feel so impregnated with damp from the garden that I don't have the strength to undress and put on my pyjamas. I burrow under the covers fully clothed, worried that I won't wake up in time in the morning.

My father must suspect that fear is my primary weakness. He is convinced that these training sessions will teach me to overcome it. Every month I have to carry out a 'meditation on death' and a 'test of courage'. They are non-negotiable. I obey without a word, never mentioning my secret terror.

My only consolation is the thought that I can go and tell Arthur all about my fears, just like I tell him about everything else: my new bedroom, the two kinds of roots, the clocks, the punishments…I talk right up close to his ear and he listens attentively. My breath must tickle him like it tickles Linda. But, unlike her, he stands stock-still as if, more than anything else, he wants to avoid interrupting me. Sometimes as I'm whispering all my misery into his ear, it gives a tiny involuntary twitch that makes my heart melt.

But Arthur is sick today; he is lying on the grass with a huge swollen belly. When he sees me he tries to stand. He is clearly too weak and slumps back down. I crouch beside him, stroke him and try to talk to him. My parents tell me to go and practise the accordion. I would like to stay, but have to obey. I try to reassure myself with the thought that I get stomach-aches sometimes too…While I struggle with my Fratelli Crosio accordion, which is unbearably heavy on my shoulders, I think about Arthur. I hope he will get better soon, and that I'll be able to see him tomorrow after lessons.

When I have finished my homework the next day, I go down to the verandah for my hour of music. It's strange, neither one of my parents is in sight. Are they waiting for me in the garden? Have I missed some instruction to go and pull up weeds? I run down the steps, happy at the thought of seeing Arthur. It's a beautiful day. I head over to where he's still lying on the grass. 'Arthur's dead,' my mother says. 'We'll have to bury him.' I don't understand. I rush over to look at him up close. And then I'm frightened. He looks so strange. Is it possible? Arthur is dead?

I turn to my father, who is sitting ten feet away on a wooden crate. My father who knows everything, can do everything. For the first time in my life I ask something of him. I ask him to bring Arthur back as he was before. He looks uncomfortable, says nothing. My mother is the one who breaks the silence.

'The vet came,' she says. 'He said Arthur ate too many apples, and that's what killed him. The vet said he was an old horse anyway; the man who sold him to us tricked us.' She goes off into an explanation about how the salesman must have blown on Arthur's gums with a straw to make him look younger.

I don't understand. I don't want to understand. I want only one thing: for him not to be dead.

'And when did the vet come?' I almost scream. 'I didn't see anyone.'

'Oh, don't you start crying now,' my mother retorts. 'If you'd looked after him he wouldn't have eaten all those apples!'

'That's enough,' my father interjects. 'Now bury him. Go and dig the hole next to the duck pond.'

Dazed, I take a spade and desperately try digging up the ground. In front of me, my mother is also digging. It's summer but the ground is very hard. I work like an automaton. There's a huge iron hand inside my chest, crushing my heart.

In the end my mother puts down her spade and says, 'We won't be able to do it.'

My father sends us off to find something to cover Arthur. All we can find is an ugly plastic tablecloth with a design of fruits and vegetables. While we secure it around his body, I find I can't take my eyes off the apples depicted on the oilcloth. The apples that killed Arthur.

All night long Linda howls desolately. All night long I cry, my heart still crushed by the steely hand.

I don't know how long Arthur has been under the tablecloth with its poisoned apples. Several days. Raymond the gardener is here this morning, leaning on his spade next to the big hole he's dug. My mother and I draw back the oilcloth. I scream. There are thousands of flies crawling over the slumped form. A hideous smell fills my lungs. I'm about to be sick.

I understand that it's over, forever. I feel like I'm falling into an abyss.

On the outside I'm still an automaton. I help by grasping one of his legs; it's so rigid it makes me shudder. But I'm not strong enough, I'm just a wisp of straw and I topple into the grave along with Arthur. Oh, the horror of that rigid body lying on me, and the suffocating stench. I fight off the flies and the cloying black earth.

'What do you think you're doing in there?' my father yells, appearing from nowhere.

No one helps me out of the hole. In the end I manage to haul myself out. I feel ashamed, dirty, stinking. And so alone. How will I live without the *clip-clop* of his hooves?

'Fill that hole in, and afterwards, Maude, you will help Raymond put the tools away in the cellar.'

No. No. No. For pity's sake, no. Not the cellar. Not Raymond. Not today. This unvoiced plea goes around and around inside my head as I trudge towards the house like an animal to the slaughterhouse. It goes around inside my head as I walk down into the cellar. It goes around while Raymond presses up behind me. While he pins me with his left arm. While he whispers in my ear, 'You loved that horse of yours,' and blows his oily breath over me. While his still muddy right hand pushes aside my clothes and worms its way into my underwear. No. No. No. Please. Please.

It's night-time. I'm in my bedroom, trying with no success to clean my underwear. I go and shut myself in the toilet, rubbing at the marks in the water inside the toilet bowl, then trying to rinse them by pulling the flush. I put them back on wet for the trip back to my room. I take them off to dry in the night, but when I put them on in the morning they're still damp. It's not the day for new underwear and I'm too dazed to get my head around secretly doing a substitution. I'll have to wear them for a few more days. I feel like they'll never dry.

The day after the burial when I go to shut Linda away in the morning, I find her coat is full of soil: she spent the night trying to dig up Arthur. She misses him as much as I do. But she thinks she can bring him back to life. My father gets us to fill the hole in again. Then he tells us to break some bottles and scatter the shards on and around the pit. A wasted effort: the next morning we find Linda covered in soil again but with her nose and paws bleeding. A few days later an electrician comes and sets up an electric fence around the grave.

Only then does Linda give up her wild hope of resuscitating Arthur.

Raymond

That wasn't the first time Raymond's dirty mitts soiled my underwear. For a long time now he's been cornering me in the cellar or the stables at every opportunity. My father calls him in one or two Saturdays a month for heavy work in the garden, pruning trees or trimming hedges. My father insists I help Raymond, as I do any workman who comes to do manual labour on the estate. 'You're thin, you can get up more easily into the loft to pass down the straw bales,' or 'Go and help Raymond fetch the tools from the cellar.' I don't see why I'm needed to fetch tools.

Raymond lurks in the cellar waiting for me. He grasps me around the waist from behind and holds me across the neck with his left arm. If I struggle or try to break away, he applies more pressure to my neck, closing my windpipe. I can't move or breathe. While he paws me with his right hand, he presses his mouth to my ear and hisses threats at me. I'm sickened by his hot, smelly breath. His right hand unzips my pants and slips inside. Or he pulls down my pants and underwear. Sometimes he completely unbuttons my top and puts his roving hands all over me.

The first time Raymond caught me in the cellar I was six years old. 'If you say anything at all,' he whispered in my ear, 'I'll kill your parents.' Did I fight him? Did I try to call for help? Either way, he obviously realized this threat wasn't dissuasive enough. He gave me his warning again, emphasizing each word, 'If you talk, I'll kill your parents. But first, I'll kill your dog.' Not Linda. He can take it out on my parents, but I couldn't bear him hurting Linda, couldn't bear for her to suffer or die because of me.

With that threat he knew he could take whatever he wanted. He reiterates it every time. There are times when he says it word for word, at others he simply says, 'Remember what I told you.'

When it happens in the cellar, he drags me over to the wall where the tools—screwdrivers, pliers, hammers, wrenches—all hang on a board with the position of each instrument outlined in white. He takes a screwdriver with a red wooden handle and trails it over my body. He often thrusts it hard into my vagina or my anus. I don't understand what he's doing, I just know it really hurts and afterwards I find blood on the toilet paper. My only means of escape is to stare at the white imprint of the screwdriver on the board. I penetrate that white silhouette on the board while the screwdriver penetrates my body.

Other times it happens in the stables. When I can tell my father is going to ask me to move some straw I run to the stables, race up the ladder and throw down the bales. I'm terrified of the mice that, disturbed by my sudden movements, scurry in every direction. But even more so of Raymond who's on his way; I can hear his carefree whistling coming closer.

Occasionally I manage to get back down before he comes through the door. Then I run as fast as I can, pushing past him and escaping his clutches. But more often than not he has already planted himself in the doorway, his predatory eyes pinned on me, revelling in the fact that he has trapped me. I feel helpless. I can't run. I can't scream. I can't cry. I'd just like to curl up into a ball in the darkest corner. His eyes take on an animal glint, his lips curl to one side in a half smile. I can feel myself falling into a bottomless pit deep inside myself.

At night he often comes back to torment me in my nightmares. I'm asleep in my room; I open my eyes and see Raymond standing by my bed with a red screwdriver in his hand. I try to scream but no sound comes out. Or I go to let Linda out in the evening but she doesn't come out. I lean in and see that she's lying there dead with a screwdriver driven into her body. Or I'm in the cellar and I've just finished doing a meditation on death. I go back up the stairs, but when I reach the door I find it won't open. I battle with the doorhandle and suddenly feel Raymond's arms grasping me from behind.

So before going to sleep in the evening I think up a thousand and one ways to kill him. Just as he's bringing the screwdriver towards me, I snatch it from him, spin around and stab it into his heart. Or I ask him to come up into the loft over the stables to help me, and as he reaches the top of the ladder I push him. He crashes to the ground and his skull splits open. Or when he's pruning the trees, I make him fall from the big ladder and he skewers himself on the shears. Or just when he's coming towards me in the cellar with that predatory look in his eye, I take out my father's shotgun. I fire once into his chest and he collapses, his face registering disbelief.

I so loathe Raymond that, apart from my murderous dreams, I try not to think about him at all. I erase him, annihilate him. He no longer exists. He has never existed.

But now Arthur is dead. Now what Raymond does to me is suddenly more than I can take. The dirt under his fingernails is Arthur's body. Arthur is dead and all my floodgates have opened. I can't pretend anymore, I can't make believe. I wish Arthur weren't dead. I wish Raymond had never touched me. I feel sad. Dirty. Dead.

Someone is howling inside me. But no one hears. No one is listening.

So where is Monsieur, my father, when this is going on, where is my shield, my defender, my guardian angel? The one who sees everything and knows everything, especially what's best for me? Who devotes every moment of his life to protecting me from the depravity of this world and the evils of the human race. Who times everything I do, even going to the toilet. Who monitors how quickly I go downstairs, every day, every time? 'You're confusing speed with haste, start again,' or 'You're thumping like an elephant, start again.' How many times have I had to go back upstairs and come down again until he finally decided I'd established the 'correct rhythm'?

Where is his legendary sense of the 'correct rhythm' now when I'm taking far longer than necessary to fetch a tool from the cellar or drop some hay bales into the stables? No one notices this, no one finds it strange. I'm overwhelmed by anger and pain.

Raymond does whatever he likes with my parents; they are his puppets. How is that possible?

When I'm allowed out into the garden I go to the spot where Arthur is buried. I make a little cross with two pieces of wood tied together, and write his name on it. I stand by his grave in private reflection. I call him. I beg him to come back. Or at least to tell me how I might join him. I'm so worried about him. If he died of a stomach-ache does that mean he still has a stomach-ache? I'm afraid he's still in pain. Or that he finds himself in the dark, frightened. I pray with all my might that, wherever he is, he is happy. I tell him that I miss him, that I love him. Since he died my days have been long, black, joyless tunnels, without hope or love.

My father is displeased by my frequent visits to Arthur's grave. He informs me that next summer a gymnasium will be built over the site. I now have to work more seriously on my physical abilities, an indispensable requirement for eventually becoming a 'superhuman'.

Whitey

I used to love the smells in the garden, the smell of shrubs, trees and flowers, of daffodils. And lilac most of all. But I don't like anything anymore. I don't like walking around the grounds. Sometimes I see Pitou, now the only free-ranging animal on the estate; he waits for me on the steps by the verandah or in the kennel with Linda. He strains his neck to see whether I'm coming out. We're having an arctic summer, drowned in rainwater. Torrents of icy water outside, streams of tears inside me.

I've read in books that people read bedtime stories to children and tuck them into bed. I'm alone, with no one to talk to. Apparently I'm a breed apart, I must stand apart. But I don't want to. Being kept apart is hell. I want to be like everyone else. I need to hold someone's hand, to be in someone's arms.

One of my favourite daydreams used to be about making

my own hot air balloon from the special fabric in the workshop, and flying away with Arthur, Linda and Pitou, just like Samuel Ferguson, the hero of *Five Weeks in a Balloon*, setting off with his companions to find the source of the Nile. Off we would go, flying over villages and countryside, over Paris and London, cities I've read about in books. From high above we would watch people getting on with their everyday lives; we would wave to them and they'd wave back.

I've stopped dreaming of travelling in a hot air balloon. Without Arthur, there's no point. Without Arthur, I'm barely alive. Life goes on around me in slow motion. Even with Linda, even with Pitou. I pretend I'm there, pretend I'm listening to what my mother's teaching me, or doing my homework or playing the accordion. I pretend to obey, to live. I'm not there. I don't know where I am. Maybe I'm nowhere.

My father mentions buying another pony, on condition that I do three somersaults on three consecutive days. In my father's world lots of things come in threes. But I don't want to do a triple somersault. And I don't want a new pony.

Days go by, blurring into each other. I feel as if my whole life is just one and the same day, an arid, endless, merciless day. I'm chained to my schedule like an ox to a cart. I pull with all my strength, but I don't understand, or think, or ask any questions. I hardly even breathe.

Weather permitting, my father regularly allocates extra chores around the grounds: weeding, lawn-mowing, clearing the gutters…the afternoon routine is turned upside down for a couple of days. 'You'll have to catch up on everything,' my father says, giving me one of his probing stares.

Catching up means my lessons are shifted around and now go on until 11:30 p.m. It means not having my brief moments of respite, like the hour of revising in the afternoon and the hour of reading in the evening, times when I can dream, secretly choose what I read, or think about those I love. Catching up means hitching a ten-ton trailer to my cart.

When there's manual labour to do, I can no longer practise my music, but the lessons with Yves still continue. I try to explain to my parents that I need time to learn the pieces. 'Excuses are for cowards and the lazy,' my parents tell me. 'Where there's a will there's a way.' However much I will my fingers to move over the required notes at the required speed, I never can. Irritated by my mediocre efforts, Yves hurls insults at me. I'm not allowed to tell him I've been working in the grounds.

The schedule is my despot and I'm its slave, all the more chained to it because I never manage to 'catch up' on the back-log. I exhaust myself trying to meet it, to complete all my tasks. There's now a constant *tick-tock* inside my head, growing louder and louder, stopping me from thinking about anything else.

I don't know whether it's because of the freezing cold summer, but a little while after Arthur's death, my teeth start chattering for no reason. I am unable to prevent my mouth from moving, but it will eventually stop on its own. Every time my jaws start quivering I have to make a huge effort to prevent anyone from hearing the *clickety-clack* of my teeth.

My mother accuses me of 'acting up'. My father inflicts a special anti-tooth-chattering exercise of willpower. Despite their protestations and punishments, I just can't stop. In the end my parents resign themselves to it, but on one condition: I chatter my teeth 'in silence'. To deaden the sound, I've taken to sucking in my cheeks so that the flesh cushions my jaws. The inside of my cheeks is now lined with a rough layer of bleeding skin. When I have an attack in the night I slip my index finger between my teeth to give the hidden wounds in my cheeks a rest.

In spite of the miserable weather, my father decides to have the greenhouse renovated. He wants to grow vines in it. Albert and Rémi come to do the work and I help by transporting bricks and cement. Given the temperature, the usual Ricard aperitif is replaced with mulled wine. The bricklayers take off their overalls at six-thirty in the evening and come onto the verandah where I pour a drink for everyone, including myself. My father watches as I fill my glass: he wants to be sure I have as much alcohol as the workmen. I drink without a word, even though I don't like the smell of the wine and hate it when my head spins.

When work on the greenhouse is finished, my father decides to extend the dovecote. I like the pigeons. It's heartwarming to see an egg one day and then find a little living creature the next. I watch the mother pigeons feed their young then settle on the nest, and I think how warm it must be under there.

Two eggs hatched a couple of days ago. One of the chicks isn't moving. His brother, a tiny featherless thing, breaks my heart with his wide little beak and clenched pink feet. He must be so sad all alone in the nest. I see him gradually grow a covering of white down, and I baptize him Whitey. I'm worried about him: he'll be flying soon and that's just when my mother likes to kill and cook them. I garner all my courage and speak directly to my father just as we are getting up from the table. 'Excuse me, Daddy...' It feels very strange calling him 'Daddy'. I only ever use the word in Father's Day letters. He must be surprised too because he turns to me, attentive. 'Daddy, can I take care of Whitey for a long time?'

I don't know how else to formulate my request. I daren't say clearly: 'Could Whitey not be killed?'

I shake as I wait to hear his verdict.

'Who on earth is Whitey?'

'A white baby pigeon. I'll take care of him. I won't take any time out of my work schedule, I'll get up earlier.'

I don't know if it's the magic of the word 'Daddy' or because, although he hasn't said so, my father understands my grief, but he says, 'Yes, if you like.' And I breathe a sigh of relief for Whitey. My heart is bereft of joy, but I'm going to look after that little ball of white fluff. Albert and Rémi probably won't need a labourer for the modest work that needs doing on the dovecote, but I'll have to go there at least twice a day to give them beers. That will be my chance to look after Whitey.

He grows up into a handsome and affectionate white pigeon who never forgets his foster mother. When he sees me in the garden he flies down onto my hand to say hello. After letting Linda out one evening, I even manage to introduce them to each other. I can tell there won't be the same connection between them as there is with Pitou, but I'm glad to know Linda will never do Whitey any harm.

Red Toothpaste

Cleanliness is not one of my father's preoccupations, so I don't have many household chores. On the rare occasions when I'm told to sweep the huge ground-floor rooms, I collect great piles of fluff. Hanging from the corners of rooms, spiders are free to weave their webs at leisure, and some create structures so enormous that we have to intervene: I fetch a special long-handled feather duster from the laundry and my father, the tallest of us, has to bring down the webs.

He may well be a knight and a great master but he's not very coordinated. He shakes the duster in every direction with his long, painfully thin hands, crushing the dusty webs and leaving trails of grey all over the walls. My mother and I silently watch the operation from a safe distance—the duster has been known to come down on our heads.

As for washing the dishes, it's quite simply a waste of time. My father has decided that at the end of meals we should just put our placemats over our plates and used cutlery, and put them with the used glasses in the sideboard in the dining room, ready for the next meal. Dishes and cutlery are washed once a week.

On the other hand, he doesn't forget to instruct us to clean the huge chandelier in the living room once every two years. My mother and I have to climb up a big stepladder and polish each piece of crystal individually. And every other year all the copper items in the house have to be burnished with Brasso.

From time to time I also have to mop the floors in the bathrooms. But no one cleans the bath or the basins, which are covered in a disgusting film of scum. According to my father, washing removes our immune defences. That is why the sheets and towels are washed only twice a year. Underwear is washed once a month. We have a sort of professional iron, but as neither my mother nor I know how to use it, we hardly ever do any ironing.

Clean laundry is hung up in the cellar where it becomes saturated with an appalling smell. Much later, as I slip between my sheets or dry myself with my towel, that smell still makes me feel sick. My parents don't even seem to notice it.

I must have an unhealthily well-developed sense of smell. I hate the smell when I hold the pot for my father to urinate into, or flush the toilet full of his excrement, or take off his socks in the evening. I hate the smell when I have to pick up rotting weeds and leaves. When I go down to the cellar I almost suffocate in the mustiness mingled with the smell of germinating potatoes and fruit stored on racks.

I watch in wonder as the ducks preen themselves, taking

forever to smooth out their feathers. Linda also licks her paws meticulously when they get dirty. One of my favourite jobs is hosing down the paving stones and seeing them come up clean and shiny. When Raymond runs his repulsive hands over me, I almost gag. I so wish I could clean my sullied skin under the hose.

There is only one exception to the general lack of cleanliness, and that is teeth. My mother is very proud of her '*dents du bonheur*'—the French expression to describe the gap in her front teeth—which is something of a distinguished feature, and she is intransigent about brushing teeth morning and evening. She is responsible for ordering toothpaste. Last year she made a mistake and a huge parcel of the brand Email Diamant was delivered. The paste is red and too runny to stay on the brush. The tube has a picture of a matador who seems to be jeering at me with his stupid smile. To my great shame, I spatter dirty specks of red over the basin, the floor and my shoes.

My mother, on the other hand, perfectly masters the matador's toothpaste, a feat that confers on her a peculiar power, especially over my father who is even more inept than I am. She glances scornfully at the results of our incompetence. After a while, I leave fewer and fewer marks, while he leaves more and more. When she sees the constellation of countless red marks on his bathmat, my mother eyes him in scornful silence. An unfamiliar expression flits over my father's face: he looks sheepish.

As a great dental specialist, my mother is always saying that tooth decay and toothaches are entirely the sufferer's fault. One day, seeing me fiddling with a tooth that is starting to come loose, she leads me off to the laundry. From the sewing box she takes some 'extra-strong' thread—once used for repairing the hot air balloons—and winds a length of it around my wobbly tooth, and ties the other end to the doorhandle. *Bam!* She slams the door, and the tooth is ripped out. I'm dumbstruck, as much by the element of surprise as by the pain.

Since then she's taken to exploring my mouth regularly. With one hand she holds my head back firmly, using the other to inspect my jaws. The day comes when she identifies another loose tooth, and decides to give it the same treatment. But this one withstands the force. She repeats the performance, slamming the door harder. The pain is blinding.

Hearing the noise, my father arrives to find quite a scene: blood streaming from my mouth and a thread dangling from the doorhandle. With a murderous look, he yells, 'Go and get the whisky, Jeannine.' My father is a great healer and whisky is his miracle remedy for anything from scrapes to toothaches. He makes me drink a good glassful, telling me to hold it in my mouth for as long as possible.

I know my mother will never pass up the opportunity to extract my other baby teeth by force, particularly as she resents me for attracting my father's attention. She is becoming obsessed with the state of my teeth. When I feel one of them starting to move, I resist touching it in front of her. But it will soon be impossible to hide it from her. I make up my mind to pull it out myself.

I steal the reel of extra-strong thread and take it out of my pocket only when everyone has gone to bed. But how to cut it? Scissors are banned from my bedroom. I rub it up and down on the edge of a drawer until it eventually wears through. Now I tie the thread to the wardrobe door and try to slam it smartly the way

I've seen my mother do it. But I can't help myself softening the blow. The tooth comes loose a bit, but doesn't come free. I have to start over, again and again. With each attempt my courage dwindles, and my anger at myself grows. I shout insults at myself in my head: 'You're just a sissy! A coward! You'll never do anything worthwhile in your life!'

I go to bed defeated. Hating my teeth, my body, hating everything about myself. As a punishment I bite my arm till it bleeds.

I don't want to go on living in fear of the day my mother finds the loose tooth. The very next morning I tell her, 'One of my teeth is wobbly.' Her face lights up. She waits until we're in the classroom, out of earshot of my father. She slams the door with one firm swing. I can see a hint of disdain in her face but it's nothing compared to the contempt I feel for my own cowardice.

The Cave

When I turn eight my father gives me an abridged edition of *Das Kapital* to study. Karl Marx is an important thinker and my father wants me to start familiarizing myself with his ideas. Why is he so important? Because he didn't merely describe the inner workings of human relationships; he dared to go further and suggest a way to make a fairer world. Of course, his ideas are utopian, but my father likes their audacity and is sorry that Freemasonry kept itself separate from any revolutionary dimension. Marx is misunderstood by most Freemasons, who see him as the devil incarnate. They are wrong, according to my father. And so, from a very young age, I am brought into contact with pure and powerful thinking that protects me from the cesspit of sheep.

This version of *Das Kapital* may well be written in simplified terms but I don't understand a word of it. I read and re-read it, but my eyes are simply scanning a succession of meaningless unconnected words. I ask my mother to explain at least the beginning. She gives me a horrified 'Certainly not! Do you want the Communists to throw us out?' Her response leaves me just as confused as the contents of the book.

I don't know whether my father realizes that my mother does not share his opinion of Marx, or of politics in general. At the moment he is very worked up, almost jubilant at the thought that Mitterrand might finally 'chuck out de Gaulle', whereas my mother seems afraid. I'm not sure I understand what's going on. Charles de Gaulle is the President of France and I think that's why his name contains a reference to France. I don't know who Mitterrand is, only that there are presidential elections going on. For the first time in a year, we finally leave the house so my parents can vote. My father insists on voting. Before getting into the car he hands a small sealed envelope to my mother and says imperiously, 'Put that in the ballot box'. He turns to me and says, 'You stay with your mother and make sure she does as I've said.' My mother doesn't look happy, but she does as she's told.

When the election results are announced, my father is furious with 'the stupid, gutless sheep who just want to keep bleating under the same shepherd'. My mother doesn't say a word, but I can tell she's gloating.

My father often talks to me about Karl Marx. 'Now you've read his work,' he says, 'you know about man's exploitation of man and you can see that the emancipation of the working class must be the work of the working class, as he puts it so well.' He often reiterates this idea. I don't understand the word 'emancipation' and dare not ask him what it means. It all seems very worrying to me, but I nod my head enthusiastically. I shudder at the thought of him discovering the full extent of my deception and stupidity. I have learnt a few passages by heart in the hope that this will be enough to fool him if he ever decides to question me on the subject.

There are other authors I have to study now: Plato, Kafka and Nietzsche. First, Plato's *The Republic*. Like my father, Plato is an Initiate. I will grow thanks to him because he will help me recognize the true light. He will stop me from being drawn to false glimmers like stupid insects drawn to electric light bulbs that kill them. I will also develop a deeper understanding of a vital concept my father has already discussed with me several times: the concept of 'the cave' and how all men are chained within its depths.

Ever since I was little, my father has told me that this cave is steeped in almost total darkness while outside all is Light, Beauty and Freedom—things that the prisoners can't see. They can see only a flickering reflection on the walls of their prison-cave. My father always ends these teachings with the words: 'That dark cave is out there, beyond our gate. In our house, though, you can enjoy the light and freedom I give you. I hope you realize how lucky you are.'

I was very impressed by these descriptions. I wondered whether there was also a cave under the village, and who were those poor people chained down there in the dark. Now, I understand that it's a metaphor for the evil of the world and man's impotence. I like immersing myself in *The Republic*. I don't understand much of it, but unlike *Das Kapital*, even the passages I don't grasp have a soothing effect, with their calm orderliness that feels full of meaning. What Plato says about Socrates makes me want to find out about him too. I ask to read his books and my mother says, 'No, you can't.' Why? No answer.

The Republic is the complete opposite of my father's chaotic teachings, which jumble terrifying ideas with episodes from his own life and horrible historical events. The last time he summoned me it was to go back over the two subjects that most obsess him: 'energies' and the Nazis. He explained what caused the downfall of the Third Reich, the most powerful regime in all history: Hitler tried to do things 'too quickly', decided to 'turn his energies in on themselves', as is clear from the swastika itself, which is merely an inversion of an ancient Indian religious symbol.

In my father's opinion, that is the worst choice anyone can make. When they spin in the right direction, energies help Beings of Light in their mission to reintegrate humanity and achieve salvation for fallen mankind. But it takes enormous time and effort to focus those energies in the right direction. When oriented the wrong way, energies can be far more powerful with even less effort. Which is why people who are in a hurry, like Hitler, like those bad roots, are tempted to reverse the direction. Those misdirected energies lead to chaos and even end up turning against those who use them.

In Hitler's entourage, there was one worthy man: Rommel. Had Hitler listened to him, the world wouldn't be where it is today. But he opted to listen to Göring, a piece of scum and a loser who thought his shit didn't stink. Göring stole works of art not because he loved art, but because he only knew how to slavishly copy the Führer, his master, in everything. Göring was the most dangerous of them all because, like all the feeble-minded, he knew how to appeal to the selfishness, stupidity and greed of the flock.

These are the despicable types I need to be wary of in the future, because they will try to destroy me. Only with extensive training can I have any hope of resisting them.

He describes other ordeals I will likely have to contend with, such as being 'tortured to get me to speak': having my fingernails torn out, my nipples clamped or burned, the soles of my feet lacerated then covered in salt. 'That's one of the reasons you have to be stronger than your body, do you see? You have to be able to suffer torture without giving them what they want to know.'

While my father talks I keep my eyes pinned attentively on his, but I can feel my mind turning to ice. I am constantly tormented by the same question: will I hold out without talking? I honestly think I won't. My father is wrong. I am not made of the stuff of superior beings. When put to the test, I am bound to disappoint him. I am already completely, hopelessly disappointed in myself.

Gregor and Edmond

Reading Kafka's *Metamorphosis*, another one of my required readings, I am horrified by Gregor's transformation. No one knows how it happens, but his nightmare becomes reality: he wakes one morning and finds he has turned into a repulsive insect overnight. I can't breathe when I think that the same thing could happen to me. I too could devolve into some abject creature, relegated to a room that gradually degenerates into a repository for all the family's filth. I find Gregor disgusting; I see myself in him. Like him I am unable to communicate, I have no companions. I feel like a cockroach, trapped in a suffocating space.

I am haunted by Gregor's fate: to be thrown into the garbage. Here I have been, dreaming naively of the adventures of Ulysses, inspired by his dazzling courage and intelligence, and delighted by his wonderful ingenuity against the Cyclops. Or dreaming of the stories by Jules Verne, whose characters—Phileas Fogg, Captain Nemo, Cyrus Smith and Samuel Fergusson—are the unforgettable heroes of my childhood. Since reading *Metamorphosis,* I keep hearing a chilling little voice inside my head saying, 'Stop dreaming. You're Gregor, you'll end up like Gregor.'

Luckily, I've managed to obtain my father's permission to read authors other than Plato-Kafka-Nietzsche in my 'free' reading hour. Alexandre Dumas, for example, whom he fortunately seems to like. He prescribes *The Mohicans of Paris* and *The Knight of Maison-Rouge.* After wading through these dark political intrigues that fail to captivate me, I take *The Count of Monte Cristo* from my father's shelves, a two-volume edition with black and white illustrations and a handsome beige binding.

I'm immediately transported. I am Edmond Dantès; we are one and the same. I feel his every emotion: his incomprehension at the monstrous punishment meted out to him; his horror at being thrown into a dungeon without knowing why or for how long; his dashed hopes; his headlong descent into rebellion, rage and despair. I am Edmond when he bangs his head against the walls, when he almost dies from being cut off from the world. Everything about the book stirs me. I experience his meeting in prison with his saviour Abbot Faria as a deliverance. The abbot cures me of my despair too, and frees me from a longing for revenge. He opens my mind to the infinite horizons of knowledge and their incalculable value. I can recite Dantès's words: 'My true treasure is your presence, it is the rays of intelligence that you have poured into my heart.'

I am Gregor, but I have found my role-model, my example, my ideal. Dantès shows me the path to freedom. When I run a trickle of cold water at night to wash my hair in secret, I'm moving away from Gregor and towards Dantès. When I see workmen from the Cathelain factory walking purposefully along the sidewalk, or hear schoolchildren laughing in the street, I'm coming closer to Dantès. Life is stronger than anything else, there is always a solution, and I will find it. I'm sure of that.

But when my father berates me, my confidence crumbles and only Gregor's world feels real. When my mother looks at me, it's not that I become Gregor, I already am Gregor, lying on my carapace, my belly exposed, ludicrously waving my little legs in the air, incapable of getting upright.

Like Edmond, I now realize my greatest handicap is ignorance. I won't be free while I have no access to true knowledge. I want to be sent to a boarding school where I'll be taught mathematics, the sciences, languages, the history of the world, geography, astronomy and the natural sciences. If all I have to feed off is the handful of subjects my mother knows—which she only grudgingly passes on—I'll be asphyxiated. I beg her to send me to a boarding school, to choose a really strict one where they teach using the cane as a threat. 'How can you betray Monsieur Didier's teaching like this?' she replies. 'You're very lucky, because I'm not even going to tell him that you've said something so shameful.'

I swallow my disappointment and avoid her gaze. I think of Abbot Faria's 'rays of intelligence'. I imagine them slicing through infinite space towards me, reaching me, caressing me with their glow, consoling me. Beneath the radiance of Abbot Faria's beams, all the nightmarish images—where I see myself locked behind the gate of the house forever or rotting in the bottom of a rubbish bin—gradually fade and eventually vanish in the immense light of intelligence.

Yesterday a whole section of the big wall around the estate fell down. 'It's because of the frost, because of this arctic winter,' declares my father. But I detect a note of anxiety in his voice, and incredulity, as if this is something that never should have happened. The masonry fell outwards. 'We'll have to clear the neighbour's field,' he says. 'But you won't be doing it, you mustn't go outside the wall.' I wonder whether he's afraid the neighbour will be angry with him. I'd love to see our neighbour, I've never seen one, and I really like the word: 'neighbour'.

Albert and Rémi, the bricklayers, are called out for the emergency. They install metal posts and run wires between them, then attach lengths of jute to the structure to fill the gaps. It's a temporary solution. While the weather remains icy, they cannot rebuild the wall. They tell us we must wait for a mild spell.

Since the wall fell down, my morning-walk-with-minimal-clothing has been cancelled, perhaps so that I won't trip over the struts, which are difficult to make out in the dark. My father is worried that the 'makeshift arrangement' won't hold, so I'm told to carry out a daily inspection at 11 a.m., before my German lesson. It is a meticulously timed mission: the return trip has to be completed within ten minutes, just enough time to cast an eye over the barrier.

Every day after my morning lessons, I head off to do my round at the far end of the grounds. When I come to the gap, I raise the corner of the tarpaulin. I could easily get through the mesh of wires. I think about it all night: if I'm quick, I could scrape for a few minutes and try to get through to the other side. By morning, I've made up my mind. I set off at a brisk pace and start running as soon as I'm out of sight.

When I reach the wall, I'm overcome with emotion. I lift the tarpaulin quickly and slip between the wires. That's it, I'm on the other side. My feet are on the hardened ground of the outside world. It's the first time I've been out alone, without my parents, almost free. I gaze transfixed; there are fields around me in every direction, as far as the eye can see. Here and there low hedges, thickets of gaunt trees. No walls, no gates, no fences. My heart swells inside my chest as if the air were better here. I take a few hesitant steps. To my right I see a little mound, I can't make out what it's made of. It's just a few paces away and I desperately want to see it close up. But the *tick-tock* of the timer inside my head tells me I don't have time; I have to get back.

I spend the whole day thinking about those funny little things piled up in the neighbouring field. I can also feel the weather getting warmer; Rémi and Albert will be rebuilding the wall soon. I must seize this opportunity to explore. The next day I run over to the gap even faster. I will be reprimanded if I go over the allotted ten minutes, but who cares, I'm consumed with curiosity.

I step over to the other side again. The air smells wonderful. I walk over to the mound: it's made up of thousands of small, shiny metallic pieces. There are lots of different shapes, lots of nuts and bolts, and also some extraordinary little coils unlike anything I've ever seen. They look like wood shavings curled up on themselves, only in metal. I pick up a perfect one, tightly sprung, and slip it into my pocket, careful not to cut myself on the sharp edges.

I breathe in the great expanse of space around me. It's such a shame that the *tick-tock* inside my head won't let me think of anything but my parents back in the house, timing my trip.

It's not long before the bricklayers come to repair the wall. First they take down the temporary barrier. I picture the gap standing naked and open, nothing blocking the way through. While the work is going on my father forbids me from going to that part of the estate.

Having thought about it, I realize that the mysterious pile most likely serves as a rubbish tip for the Cathelain factory nearby, that those pieces of metal are waste. This does nothing to diminish the value of my precious little shaving, which I keep carefully hidden in the lining of my bedroom curtain. Sometimes, when I'm alone in the evening, I take it out to look at it. It reminds me of that glorious, intoxicating escapade, which was as magical as it was unhoped for.

The Orange Book

The upkeep of the garden takes a lot of work: digging, planting vegetables, picking fruit, repainting fences. My mother and I devote many hours to it. The most monotonous chore is weeding. My mother has special gloves ordered from the Manufrance mail-order catalogue so, in theory, she's the one who is supposed to pull out the thistles. But, depending on my father's mood, I am sometimes told to do it. I work with my bare hands. I make every effort to grip the thistles right down at the root, but I'm not very good at it and my hands often get covered in prickles.

My father never lifts so much as his little finger. He 'directs' and 'monitors' our labours, presiding from his crate, a wooden box with the word 'Libourne' stamped on it, once used for transporting wine. When he feels we're too far away from him, he cries, 'Maude, the crate!' I have to hurry back, pick up the crate and move forward until he says: 'Stop!' Then he sits back down.

Over time, the instruction has become increasingly clipped. Now he simply says, 'Crate!' But his voice still strikes me like a lightning bolt.

My father is very keen on the electric fence erected around Arthur's grave to prevent Linda from trying to dig up the pony. He has electric fences put along all the walkways, aiming to 'discipline everyone'. I think his main aim is to stop 'outsider' animals coming and frolicking freely in the grounds, particularly stray cats, which he loathes. My father thinks cats are traitors, evil creatures that rob us of our energies. He tells me that any cats venturing onto our land will get caught because, even though they can pass freely under the fencing, their tails will inevitably touch the electric wires and they'll get a decent shock.

Soon the whole estate is crisscrossed with these wires. In certain places, the fences have up to three rungs of wire, one above the other. In order to make them a more effective trap for intruders, my father gets us to paint the posts with green Ripolin paint, as camouflage.

When I pick up fallen branches I now have to work around these fences. Any branches that touch both the fence and the ground give off an annoying *tsit-tsit-tsit-tsit*. One day, while pulling up weeds near a stand of trees, I am not careful enough and get an electric shock. I scream. My father jumps in surprise, almost falling off his crate. 'Idiot, moron, good-for-nothing, sissy!' he bellows furiously. He orders me to grab the wire in both hands and hold it until he allows me to let go. I brush my fingers over the wire but snatch them back straightaway, terrified by the steely taste in my mouth and by my racing heartbeat. I try again several times without success. Beside himself, my father works himself into such a towering rage that I end up grasping the wire in my fist. I don't know how many seconds go by. All I know is the shocks are unbearable.

My father snaps at me that from now on I'll have a new 'electric fence' test as part of my tests of willpower. Every day, or at least twice a week, I'll have to hold the electric fence for ten minutes without betraying any feeling, no twitching or grimacing, not even a blink. I soon find I actually cope quite well. It's just a question of tolerating what is, of course, an unpleasant feeling but at least it is a known quantity. I would willingly swap a whole day on the electric fence for a single session of meditating on death in the cellar—a test that still leaves me just as devastated as the first time.

My progress on the will-strengthening front is too slow, so my father bolsters my training with other exercises. Like the 'spinning' test which takes place near the swimming pool, in the 'rotunda', a raised pergola built where two cement paths meet. I have to stand in the middle, close my eyes and, on my father's order, start turning on the spot, faster and faster like a spinning top. I have to make sure I stay right in the centre of the circle. As soon as I hear 'Stop! Exit to the right' or 'Exit to the left' I have to walk steadily down the appropriate path.

My efforts are hopeless. I feel giddy, my temples pound frantically, my legs give way, I start to shake with anxiety. When the order to stop comes, I try to walk straight but usually stagger and knock into the balustrade. Then I know I've failed and I'm overwhelmed with panic. I can't even look around to establish right from left. My father is very displeased. 'Don't go thinking you'll get away with this,' he says. 'We'll keep going till you get it right, it's just a question of willpower.'

I feel terribly ashamed. It's not exactly rocket science. Maybe I have something wrong with my brain and my father is trying to cure it. The spinning test is one of the tests that leave me feeling extra sad. In my bed at night I picture myself succeeding at it; I concentrate and manage the perfect exit. But however hard I try in reality, I fail, and it becomes more and more distressing.

This year my father introduces a new anti-celebration ritual for my ninth birthday. On the morning of my birthday, he summons me to the largest room, a place so cold this time of year that we rarely set foot in it. He makes me sit down in front of an orange mathematics book, gives me a list of problems to solve and leaves me there on my own. No getting up until I've finished. Just reading the first one makes my head spin: 'Town A and town B are 20 km apart. At 10 a.m. Monsieur X sets off by train from A to B. The train travels at a constant speed of 60 km/h. At 10:10 Monsieur Y sets off by bicycle from B towards A and travels at a constant speed of 15 km/h. At what time do Monsieur X and Monsieur Y pass each other?' There's also a question about a cyclist who changes speed for part of the journey, another about a leaking tap and a basin filling up...

Hard as I try, I can't find even the beginnings of a solution. I'm not allowed to cry, not allowed to leave and not allowed to ask for explanations. I can feel myself growing more stupid by the minute. Hours go by; I try different operations and scribble various figures. I move on to the next question, thinking I'll come back to this one later, but the second gives me an equally hard time.

I'm starting to get thirsty, but I know I won't be allowed to eat or drink until I've finished. Mealtimes come and go. It's getting late in the evening. It's 10 p.m. already. I make up my mind to submit my work to my father. He glances at it then turns his steely eyes on me. 'Do you really think this is right?' he asks. 'If you think it's right leave it with me. But if you've made any mistakes, you'll have three extra problems to solve for each mistake. It's up to you.' I quickly take back the sheet of paper and go back to work.

Around midnight my mother says, 'Go to bed. You can finish in the morning. Your father will let you have some breakfast, but that's all.' I have a feverish night's sleep, haunted by trains and bicycles barrelling towards each other. The next morning, I sit down to the orange book again. The only interruption I'm granted is the forty minutes during which I attend to my father. I rack my brain, scour it, spur it on. At the end of the day, when I've written the exercises out neatly, I agonize about handing them to my father. I know he's going to ask, 'Do you think it's right?' And do I think it's right? No, I really don't…

I have another night of torment and wake feeling terrible, forced to face the orange book again in my zombie-like state. After an interminable length of time, my father finally decides to suspend the test. He closes the orange book and says, 'We'll come back to this next year. We'll see whether between now and then you can learn to use your brain.'

Cuvée 1945

My parents' philosophy on the subject of sickness can be summarized in one line: 'Being sick doesn't exist. It's all in your head. Get up!' Except when this thing that only exists in weak people's minds gets to my father. Then all activity stops immediately. The constant treadmill of my schedule grinds to a halt. My mother and I go into my father's bedroom, close the door and draw the double drapes. And we stay there motionless in silence, in the dark, in the stale air and the unbearable stuffy smell until he feels better. As I'm not allowed out, Linda is not shut in from eight in the morning till eight in the evening. Even mealtimes are all over the place. We have to wait until my father feels like eating.

He usually asks for rice cooked with lots of sugar. My mother goes and makes enough for the three of us. We have to eat exactly the same food and drink the same drinks as him. We hold his plate while he eats. He spatters his sheets and we clean them up before eating our own food at the desk. Sometimes he wants a hot toddy made with cognac, and my mother brings up three glasses on a tray.

I'm in charge of the chamber pot, so I can't go anywhere. I'm also responsible for monitoring his breathing, which has to be nice and 'regular'. I'm not too sure what that means. And I don't know what I should do in the event of a problem. I imagine he would tell me himself. But from time to time he falls asleep and then his rasping breath frightens me. I go over and look at him close up, slightly disgusted by the beginnings of a greying beard on his chin. I hate myself for this reaction; I'm a bad daughter.

At night, one of us sleeps in the armchair, the other on the desk chair, our heads resting on our folded arms. We swap places sometime in the night. The most difficult thing is going to the toilet. Neither of us dares ask permission to go. We exchange fur-tive glances in the half-light until he releases us by asking for his pot. My mother takes the opportunity to slip away to the toilet, and I take my turn when I empty the pot.

Our task is to 'watch over' him, there is no question of our doing anything else, no reading, writing, drawing, tidying, chatting...The hot toddies I drink knock me out a little. And the immobility gives me stabbing cramps. Time seems to pass appallingly slowly. At the end of the third day, one of us goes out to check that everything's all right in the house and garden, and to feed the animals.

One time we stayed shut inside for more than a week. I remember the strange feeling that I was imploding, then I was filled with a torpor that could have gone on indefinitely.

As soon as my father is better, he insists we 'catch up' on all the hours we've lost 'doing nothing'.

Despite his giant frame, my father has a fragile constitution. He has asthma, and the chill that hovers over the barely heated house causes him frequent bouts of bronchitis. I struggle to understand how the fearsome superior being he is, this knight, this master of willpower who can dominate the world with his sheer strength of mind, should feel so unwell that he can't get out of bed. Could it be my fault? Does he need to 'recharge his energies' regularly because he is exhausted by the considerable efforts he expends training someone as inadequate as me?

By contrast, my mother is solid as a rock and stays on her feet even when she has the flu. Only twice has she had to take to her bed with a high fever. My father then took charge of everything. He went to the kitchen, a room in which he never normally sets foot, and showed me how to make a hot toddy: heat a good measure of cognac, add a couple tablespoons of sugar and an egg yolk. The mixture looked revolting, and I saw my mother's eyes roll in disgust as she drank it.

As for me, because I'm training to be a superhuman, sickness is inadmissible. If I ever have a stomach-ache, toothache or headache, it's as if I've done something wrong. If I really have a very high temperature, my father gives me a couple of aspirin.

The same goes for pain; I'm not allowed to feel it. One time, when we were doing some building work, I fell onto a beam bristling with nails that drove into my leg. My father poured half a bottle of whisky over the area, making sure it got right into the puncture wounds that were spewing blood. 'I'm sacrificing half a bottle of Johnnie Walker Red Label for a silly little injury. I hope you realize how much you mean to me and appreciate the expense I'm going to.'

I can still feel my tongue pressing on the roof of my mouth, my limbs stiffening. It took an enormous effort to stifle my screams.

But sometimes I'm so sick that it's hard for anyone to dismiss it as 'acting up'. In winter, I get tonsillitis so badly I feel I have a pair of ping-pong balls at the back of my throat, and I'm delirious with fever. My father, who is always quick to point out that he is 'the best doctor on the planet', treats me with a special remedy which he keeps exclusively for me: a tin of tuna in oil, with a good slug of 1945 vintage white wine. The oil makes me feel nauseous, the flakes of tuna get trapped between my tonsils and my throat hurts so much it's difficult to swallow. The dark yellow, syrupy liquid reminds me of my father's urine in the pot. But I soon forget about this because I'm more interested in the sight of my father leaning incredibly close to me as he spoonfeeds me and holds my glass for me as I struggle to swallow.

I can't believe my eyes: he never worries about me, yet here he is going to such trouble, being so patient, almost gentle, even looking concerned. As if I've suddenly become someone very precious who must be saved at all cost. It's too much of a contrast with my day-to-day life. My head is spinning in amazement, while the rest of my body succumbs to giddying fever.

The 1945 vintage white wine must be working. I spend most of my time in a deep cloying sleep, emerging from the fog only when I hear my father's footsteps. The moment he comes into the room he fills every inch of it. I automatically hold my breath. Then I remember I'm sick and my father is my doctor today. 'You're going to be fine, little gal,' he says in a strangely gentle voice I've never heard before. I can tell he feels awkward, and I'm not very taken with that 'little gal'. But it's the only sign of tenderness he can manage, the only one he'll offer me, and, oh Lord, it's better than nothing! For a fleeting moment I look into his anxious eyes, then we're both quick to look away.

He brings a hand to my face, rests his unusually long fingers on my forehead and checks my temperature. Every ounce of me hopes he will stroke my cheek. Just one caress with the tips of his fingers, and the house would disappear, the gates and walls would vanish, we would be outside, happy and free. But the caress never comes. His fingers have left my forehead. And the next minute he breaks the spell by yelling towards the doorway, 'She's awake, Jeannine. Bring the white wine!'

From Underground

Alcohol is now an important part of training my willpower. Since I was seven or eight, my father has insisted I have an aperitif and drink wine at mealtimes. The mind is stronger than anything else so I have to learn to hold my drink. Besides, difficult negotiations in life often go hand in hand with consuming large quantities of alcohol, so those who can handle their drink will prevail. It's also really useful for getting information out of someone: I could encourage them to drink, drink with them, then after a few glasses they would be drunk and in my power. Because my head would still be clear.

Likewise, after competitions of bottoms-up, I have to be able to handle a gun in case I get into a duel. I wonder how on earth I could be dragged into a duel, but daren't ask him. Duels may be the sort of thing I'll have to face later, when I'm a knight.

As I grow up, I have to get used to putting away more and more alcohol. At noon I have to have a glass of Ricard with water before lunch. Then a generous glass of white wine during the meal, followed by a glass of red. And cognac to finish. We have only fifteen minutes for the meal so these drinks have to be knocked back swiftly.

My father claims that Ricard is an excellent remedy for any kind of infection, especially in the mouth. He occasionally makes me drink it neat. The smell alone feels like a rocket about to explode inside my head. The first sip burns my gums, then the fire travels down my throat and blazes into my stomach.

And that's not all. We now have to start specific 'alcohol and willpower' training, carried out every month or two. For the purposes of this exercise, my mother and I have had to paint two long white strips—15 inches wide by 10 metres long—onto the cemented parts of the garden. The exercise entails downing a glass of undiluted Ricard, swiftly followed by a glass of whisky and sometimes a glass of cognac, then walking steadily the length of the 10-metre strip without stepping outside the line. I cling to that line with all my might. I don't know how I manage it, but I seem to succeed in this exercise quite frequently.

I hate alcohol and I hate the smell of neat Ricard most of all. Obviously, I don't mention this to my father, who thinks everyone—women, children, workmen—should drink as much as he does. My father attributes all sorts of benefits to alcohol, but I remember the ravaged alcoholics I've come across in literature: Dimitri from *The Brothers Karamazov*, the heartbreaking heroes of *L'Assommoir*. I'm obscurely aware that I would be in grave danger of losing myself if alcohol 'took hold of me'. It's mostly for my own sake that I concentrate so hard and outperform myself in these tests. I don't need another 'master'. I want to learn to stand up to alcohol, not so that I can manipulate or crush opponents, but to allow Abbot Faria's beams of intelligence to reach me.

I sustain myself on images of salvation, and strong, charming heroes. I have an increasingly powerful need for books, which throw a glimmer of light into my darkness. Whenever I have a moment to myself, I scour my father's bookshelves. I find Zola, Maupassant, Daudet. My mother never reads novels and certainly not popular fiction; she raises her eyes to the heavens when my father sings the praises of Alexandre Dumas, and has the lowest opinion of Eugène Sue. I'm enchanted by Eugène Sue's *The Mysteries of Paris* and adore Rodolphe, always ready to defend the widows and orphans: 'I've suffered already in my own life; that explains my compassion for those who suffer.' He takes me with him deep into the world of crooks and burglars. I'm touched when he can see good in the hearts of those 'fallen wretches'.

When I discover *The Idiot,* it feels like I've stumbled onto a gold mine. I develop a passion for Dostoyevsky. I'm fascinated by all his characters. They're so alive, so three-dimensional, such a mess! Exactly the opposite of the 'perfect beings' my father so loves; they literally throb with life. They hate, they love, they're filled with enthusiasm. They stumble and struggle with mental chaos. They ask themselves endless questions, don't think about their answers, and forge ahead with their longings and whims and mistakes. They're exhaustingly beautiful. Dostoyevsky shows me that life is even more terrible than my parents have told me, full of violence, humiliation, revenge, betrayal…But still so worth living! Far from fearing life, being suspicious of it or erecting walls against it, his characters cherish it, dive headlong into it, and drown in it if need be. 'Everything is worth living,' they seem to tell me. 'Stop being afraid.'

If my mother leaves the classroom for any length of time, I like to slip into the next room, which we use as a storeroom. It's forbidden, but I love rummaging through the boxes, even if there's nothing particularly exciting in them: bedcovers, old newspapers, the odd book. One day I come across a Dostoyevsky I haven't seen before: *Notes from Underground.* I have time to read only a few pages. I can't take it to my bedroom; that would betray my unauthorized exploring. I hide it under a pile of old tablecloths. I return to it over successive days, reading three or four pages at a time, caught up in the maelstrom of contradictory thoughts buffeting this extraordinary hero, who is frenetic, evil, bitter, selfish, tormented, cowardly…He's cantankerous, he's a loser who takes revenge for the slights he feels he has suffered, by pretending to be magnanimous with Liza, a young prostitute. He even gives her his address in case she wants to redeem herself.

When Liza comes to find him, he walks all over her. But she guesses the terrible suffering that lies beneath his loathsome behaviour, and offers herself to him. For a moment, he is thrown by her generosity, wishing he could believe it. But his demons soon regain the upper hand. She forgives him, but she flees.

I'm so shaken by the story that I read it over and over, still in secret, and still in small snatches. Over time, I come to understand that this hero who so moves me reminds me of my father. They share an impulse to reject other people, the world and its conventions; they have the same frenzied conviction, harshness and tendency to speechify…I wonder whether my father is also hiding an open wound beneath his inflexible exterior. Could it be that everything he says, thinks, does and insists on, that this whole world in which he imprisons us might actually be the result of some secret suffering of his, and not related to a higher understanding at all?

With every new reading, I'm gripped by the ending's harsh lessons. 'Don't expect anything of him,' it seems to be telling me. 'Even if someday he realizes his own folly, he is dangerous and beyond redemption. Get out!'

The Pyramid

I sit motionless and silent, completely focused on a fork in front of me on the dining-room table. My mother is sitting opposite me, carrying out the same exercise. At the head of the table, my father issues his instructions in his deep voice: 'Focus on the metal. Get psychically inside it. Take hold of it psychically. Now make it move. Push it.'

I'm taut as a bow, I can't even breathe. Please move, metal, please. I'm going cross-eyed looking at this fork, I'm seeing double, triple; sometimes I even see it slide. But it's not twisting, it's not doing what my father wants. I can hear my mother's breathing, calm and regular, while I'm in a state of apnoea. I'm frightened of failing. My father's eyes are on me; it feels as if he's delving right into my mind, getting inside my head.

I suddenly see the fork change shape. I did it! Then I relax the focus of my eyes and take a proper look. Now it looks just the same as it always was. And so does my mother's. I'm disappointed.

My father tells me that at first the fork will just quiver. That is to be expected because I don't yet know how to keep my mind under control. In fact, the metal did move very slightly, he says, but my mind was too inexperienced to notice it and is therefore still focusing on the same point. It is this discrepancy that causes the fork to jitter. The next stage, when I've learned to stabilize my 'hold', will be for me to move the whole thing. The hardest part is 'achieving the first movement'. Once you have mastered that, the rest comes naturally.

Another variant of this exercise involves getting the hands to move on a watch that hasn't worked for years. My mother thinks she's very good at this game. She triumphantly shows us her watch hand, which has moved from 10 o'clock to 10.01. It's a really small watch and the hands are quite hard to make out, but I'm almost sure she's right. As with the fork, the hand dances before my straining eyes and I sometimes feel as if I've succeeded in making mine move too. At times I even think I've made it go backwards! Maybe I've practised so much that my mental powers have succeeded in controlling solid matter. Or maybe I've spent so long looking at those tiny hands that my eyes start seeing things that aren't there. I don't know but, despite his failing eyesight, my father is in no doubt. He inspects our watches and nods his head approvingly, which floods me with relief. I don't fully understand but, seeing as he looks pleased…

I enjoy these hour-long exercises in mental concentration that require a profoundly calm atmosphere. For those sixty minutes I can be sure I won't hear any yelling. And I certainly prefer them to the 'nail' exercises that were my first training in dominating solid matter. One day my father gave me a thick wooden plank into which my mother had driven a nail with a single hammer blow. The exercise consisted in driving the nail in further by hitting it every day with the palm of my hand. It did eventually happen after several months, and at the cost of a big gash in the middle of my palm. I admit I didn't see the point of that exercise.

My father never stoops so low as to bend a single fork or move the hands of a watch. Those are exercises for 'apprentices'. He has reached such heights in mental power that he could fold the Eiffel Tower in two if he wanted. But, of course, he would do no such thing because the Eiffel Tower is a symbol and a reference point for all Beings of Light: 'Because of course, it's a pyramid that shines a light from its summit,' he explains. Besides, Gustave Eiffel was a Freemason and a great Initiate, just like Auguste Bartholdi, whose Statue of Liberty brandishes…what? A torch. What people don't know is that these two edifices also serve another purpose, relaying vibrations and therefore allowing Beings of Light to connect through them to the axe of pure energy. Thus when Beings of Light are regenerating, this purity is diffused throughout the universe.

I'm astounded by the complexity of things around me, and the processes going on without my realizing it. To think that I can be dazzled by butterflies, birds and other such inanities. My parents are right to call me a 'village idiot'.

There is one thing I have managed to grasp and remember from my father's many teachings: it was the Egyptians, particularly the high priests of Memphis, who discovered the special capacity of pyramidal structures to concentrate light and vibrations, as in worship of Ra, the God of Light. Geometry generally modifies the circulation of energies. Of all geometric forms, pyramids are best equipped to 'sustain the life' of the newly deceased pharaoh. We need only remember the Masonic triangle, the first geometric form, and the pyramid which represents its three-dimensional elevation. This ternary acts as a generator of life, renewal and reincarnation, the exact opposite of the process of dying.

All the pharaohs are supremely enlightened beings who knew how to make the transition from the world of the living to the world of the dead: their servants, pets and wives were entombed with the mummy to help the master continue his life in the heavenly Field of Reeds while the young pharaoh perpetuated his work on earth. What the uninitiated don't realize is that the pharaohs can make the journey in reverse should the need arise. They have fathomed the mysteries of the universe, and can reveal them or obscure them at will.

The teaching sessions about Egypt are held in the grandest part of the house, the vast billiard room. Occasionally I'm summoned to a room where we rarely set foot: the sitting room. My father is convinced that it transmits waves from the previous occupiers of the house, three ageing spinster sisters who spent their final years cloistered in this family room. They died there one after another, the survivors watching over the dead until the last one left this world and, according to my father, her spirit is still 'trapped' in the room. When we are in there he wears different coloured strings around his neck attached to a metal triangle on the end. I have to wear the same thing but with a white string.

He takes a wooden box from the bookshelves. From inside, he produces a dollar bill, on which he shows me the famous truncated pyramid in the centre of the great seal. The beaming triangle which crowns the pyramid is in fact the vibratory call of the God Ra. The founders of the United States who designed the bill, all Freemasons and outstanding Initiates, had the ingenious idea of including the call of Ra on banknotes as a way of 'harvesting the vibrations' of all that touched them.

Hardly surprising, then, that the United States is the most competent country in the world. My father doesn't disguise his admiration for the country's organisation, diligence and efficiency. When he talks about it, he stands taller and a note of pride comes into his voice, as if he himself were American. France, on the other hand, inspires only his contempt: 'The Gauls were just a tribe of disorganized savages and Vercingetorix was a cretin. How could the French be anything but stupid...?' He often compares nations with this parable: when something needs doing the French say 'I'm going to do it' without ever actually getting on with it; the Germans say 'I'm doing it' as they get on with it; the Americans, who don't speak until the task is completed, say 'I've done it.'

Despite all this, contrary to popular belief and even though he's a high-ranking Mason, the American President is not the most powerful man on the planet. The true masters of the world are two other Freemasons: first, the Queen of England in her capacity as historic patron of Freemasonry, and second, the hidden supreme master who steers the business world as well as the spiritual world: the Pope. The Vatican has also perfected a unique system for harvesting the vibrations from a maximum number of people. Using the traditional Papal address, *urbi et orbi*, the Pope stands in a dominating position, looking out over all of Saint

Peter's Square, and performs a special gesture, which the faithful take to be a blessing but which is in fact a way of drawing in and appropriating the energy of the thousands of followers gathered beneath his balcony.

The Pope's role as supreme overlord does not mean that the entire Church is made up of Initiates—far from it. Priests, who enjoy a degree of power, are mostly contemptible individuals with lowly, impure souls—which makes them dangerous. As for the believers, they are nothing but a vast flock of sheep perfectly unaware of what is really going on. In passing, my father always warns me to be wary of crowds, because individual energies are weakened when they come into contact with others, especially powerful people who know how to suck the lifeblood out of you and use you to their own ends. If I ever find myself in a large gathering, it's crucial that I find some way to position myself above it if I'm to avoid this diluting process.

There is, of course, another superior group of people: not the Christians but the Jews. Having always been persecuted, they have to play their cards close to their chests, passing themselves off as losers, skinflints. In fact, while those who are not persecuted have slowly turned into 'great spineless masses' obsessed with their own comfort, the Jews have developed a keen intelligence, a remarkable capacity for cooperation and, most importantly, the sense of secrecy without which nothing valid can ever be achieved.

Rabbis, who are a thousand times more intelligent than Catholic priests, have been learning how to harness energies since the dawn of time. They use in particular the seven-armed menorah candelabra. Having inherited their magic from ancient Egypt, the rabbis have been careful to keep this traditional source active and their sacred scriptures alive. Some rabbis are great alchemists, and they pass on their art with utmost secrecy. This is why Hitler embarked on exterminating the Jews: the swastika that he had inverted—and thus rendered uncontrollable—was beginning to escape his grip, and he feared that it might fall into the hands of rabbis who would have made much better use of it than him.

My father says that our family is descended from Jews. He occasionally mentions a great-aunt Sarah and a great-uncle Samuel. I've never met them and don't know whether they're still alive. In any event, having given so much help to Jews during the war, my father is now considered 'one of them', and it is actually thanks to them that he made his fortune. 'As my daughter, you could ask for their help, should you ever need it later in life. Remember that.' I carve this information into my memory. The only problem is I don't know where to find them, and my father never tells me how to contact them.

The Tiger Rug

Unlike the grounds, where new construction work is undertaken every summer, the inside of the house never changes. An ornament atop a piece of furniture might as well be glued there for all eternity. On her way out of my lesson one day, my mother stops dead in front of the Persian rug in the middle of the corridor. In a flash of inspiration, she says, 'It would look better down on the first-floor landing.' I can't make out her tone of voice; it's almost as if she were asking my opinion. For a moment I'm stunned; no one has ever asked what I think of anything. Then, suddenly excited at the thought of introducing even such a negligible change into my repetitive existence, I nod vigorously.

Ever since I was very young, I've liked this rug, with its lithe, majestic tigers on a red background. It reminds me of the days when we still lived in Lille, before we shut ourselves away in this prison. I can remember my father talking to me in an astonishingly gentle voice, saying, 'If you look closely at the pattern—that tiger there, for example—if you keep your eyes focused on it, you'll see it move.' And the tigers in that rug really did move before my eyes. Now I can't wait to move the rug itself.

We each pick up one end of the rug. It's incredibly heavy and we can't slide it along the floor because it drags on the wall-to-wall carpet underneath. When my mother tries rolling it up, she topples over several times. I suppress the urge to laugh; my father—sitting in the dining room as usual—mustn't hear us. But we both succumb to hysterical laughter. I'm sure that, like me, she's thinking about an incident involving the actor Maurice Chevalier and the entertainer Mistinguett, a story my father tells us to illustrate the dangers of contact between people of the opposite sex. Maurice Chevalier and Mistinguett performed a show together during which they would both emerge from a large carpet that was unrolled on the stage. One day when the carpet unfurled too quickly, the astonished audience were confronted with…the couple locked in a passionate kiss. 'And to think they were both in separate relationships!' my father always concludes reprovingly.

It takes us a ridiculously long time to get the rug as far as the staircase. There the problem worsens: we have no idea how to get it down the first flight, and even less how to get it around the half-landing to go down the second. 'Let's tip it over the banister,' my mother whispers. We haul it laboriously over the banister rail and—*wallop!*—there it is a floor below, still balancing on the banister and threatening to continue its fall. We scurry down on tiptoe, just managing to catch it before it slumps to the ground floor.

The panic! We narrowly avoided a disaster: the rug very nearly knocked over the bronze statue standing in pride of place at the foot of the stairs. That statue is my father's mascot: Athena holding the sphere of knowledge in her left hand. I have been treated to several teaching sessions on the subject of this statue. Why the left hand? Because that is the chosen hand of the Initiates. Why a sphere? It is a symbolic shape representing knowledge, the world of ideas as defined by Plato, but it is also the perfect geometric form comprising an infinite number of triangles as well as the 'magic square of the wise'.

My father thinks everything is symbolic and he attributes extraordinary value to basic geometric shapes such as triangles and squares, claiming they carry within them a tiny portion of the primordial energy of creation. Understanding and respecting these shapes is the first step towards learning to set the energies spinning in the right direction and, therefore, to having a chance of accessing occult philosophy. He offers no explanation of the magic square of the wise, and I don't dare ask. I picture a gathering of great Initiates sitting in a square formation and discussing the universe and its energies.

My mother and I eventually position the rug on the first floor and hurry back upstairs to study for what little time is left. When we come back down at the end of the afternoon, we walk past our rug and agree: it looks much better here. All the same, we are apprehensive about how my father will react when he sees it on his way to bed.

The time for the evening procession comes at last. We climb the stairs in single file, my mother leading to soften the fall should he stumble forwards, and me bringing up the rear in case he falls backwards. The tiger rug lies bathed in the lamplight right in the middle of the first-floor landing. My father walks over it and goes into his bedroom without a word. We exchange anxious glances behind his back. Still no reaction during the bedtime routine. We go back out into the corridor stunned, and head off to bed. He will realize tomorrow.

After his morning ritual the next day, we follow him along the landing, both tense. The excitement of the previous day has abated. We walk over the rug one behind the other, and reach the stairs. Still no comment. We go downstairs in the prescribed order with me at the front and my mother behind. Nothing. Not a word.

A week passes by like this. Day after day we wait for him to reprimand us. But nothing of the sort happens. As we head upstairs one evening my mother cracks. Either to bring an end to what has become unbearable apprehension, or because she doesn't have it in her to hide even the smallest thing from him. 'Monsieur Didier,' she starts hesitantly, 'You'll see we have moved a rug onto the first floor…' She doesn't have time to finish her sentence. My father leaps up the stairs and, seeing the rug, flies into a towering rage: 'This is unacceptable! Put things back as they were, immediately!'

Easier said than done. Our legs wobbling with the strain, we drag the rug an inch at a time. Every now and then we hear my father's furious footsteps as he strides to his bedroom door, yanks it open and bellows: 'What the hell are you doing? Haven't you finished yet?'

We manage somehow to get the rug back up to the second floor. Hanging our heads in shame, we finish waiting on my

135

father and return to our rooms without making eye contact.

The next day he decides to do a general inspection of the house to check we haven't moved anything else. He storms from room to room and we follow in silence. He seems to find objects that have been moved all over the place and interrogates us aggressively. Luckily, the thick layer of dust corroborates our answers. In the end—because we clearly have time on our hands—he punishes us with new chores. My mother has extra accountancy exercises to complete and I have to copy out the whole of Dandelot's *Practical Guide to the Musical Keys*.

This seems to me a light punishment for the week of exciting complicity I've just had with my mother. We did something to brighten our humdrum existence, we shared a secret, harboured the same concerns, the same fears, the same tension. And my mother doesn't hold me responsible for the failure of our venture, which makes me feel almost lighthearted.

I sometimes think about the journey those tigers made. Now I feel like moving everything around, furniture, ornaments, books…turning everything upside down, even the schedule. As if the door of change has been thrown open, and I've worked out how to stop our fates being sealed once and for all. How wonderful life would be if my mother and I were friends and could dream up other adventures. If we could defy my father's increasingly oppressive authority with other little schemes.

Hiram of Tyre

'I am not from any time or of any place; beyond time and place, my spiritual being lives in eternal existence.' This is how my father likes to describe himself. In his teaching sessions, which relate more and more to 'fundamental issues', he explains that he has already lived many lives and met other Beings of Light. He benefitted from the teachings of Pythagoras, one of the great founders of the secret doctrine. He took part in the crusades wearing the armour of the Knights Templar. He was a Cathar 'perfectus'. In the difficult era of the French Revolution—during which he was incarnated as Giuseppe Balsamo, who became famous under the alias of Count Alessandro Cagliostro—he was a disciple of another great Initiate, the Count of Saint-Germain...

Perhaps as a result of these multiple incarnations, my father is a 'thaumaturgist', a miracle-worker; he can heal simply through the laying on of hands, like Saint Louis and the Merovingian kings from whom we're descended. 'We are Didiers, the direct descendants of the 'Do-nothing kings', we're pure,' he often tells me. He explains that the commonly misunderstood term 'do-nothing' derives from the fact that these enlightened kings didn't waste their energies on menial activities like walking. They travelled in ox-drawn carts, which meant they could contemplate higher matters. Because this behaviour had no 'concrete, visible or immediate' results, lesser mortals interpreted it as laziness. The world was not ready for their wisdom. Yet they achieved great things in the invisible universe and their impact would be understood later, in the fullness of time.

My father can also use a Ouija board, in other words, commune with the dead. For example, he talks to his mother in the hereafter. I must not confuse these authentic powers of his with the demonstrations put on by 'apprentice psychics' who can only communicate with 'freak-show ghosts'. The sheep are awestruck by these performances and that's just as well, because it leaves the truly chosen free to converse with higher spirits. Similarly, I should not be impressed by people who turn lead into gold: that's just 'small potatoes', within the skill set of the lowliest 'novice alchemist'.

Great Initiates like my father have far more formidable abilities, such as penetrating other people's minds. They can also control people by hypnotizing them. 'I can do absolutely anything with any weak mind,' my father is forever claiming. By definition these people have no power over their own minds. In contrast, strong minds fully master their mental energies and can therefore enter other people's minds and manipulate them like puppets just as easily as they can resist pain and inebriation or bend metal and move inanimate objects. Hypnotism is a powerful instrument, and a lasting one: you need only 'put someone under' once and they will still be in your control years later.

My father assures me that he has never hypnotized me and never will. As I'm destined to become a superhuman myself, I mustn't be subject to any form of mental possession. Once my training is complete, I will control the weak-minded and bring about the great regeneration of the universe.

I have no desire to control anyone. Does being strong mean living cloistered in this house like my father? Well, then, I'd rather have a weak mind and live like the factory workers at the Cathelain plant. If, however, I'm condemned to fulfilling my father's expectations, to 'get inside people's heads', then I'll use my power to free these so-called weak minds. I picture myself opening a metal gate, but instead of going in and taking possession of anyone, I hold the gate open so all those captive souls can escape. The fantasy gives me the same sweet feeling as when I open the door to Linda's kennel. Never mind if I risk being trampled by the crowds of people racing to get out. In my imaginary scenario I see myself dying with a smile on my lips, proud to have given others their freedom…

I have never seen my father commune with spirits, read the future in cards, or control someone he has hypnotized. That's to be expected: he's such a fully realized being that he no longer needs to prove anything. I don't know how he acquired his powers, whether he once had teachers who patiently trained him. I figure his gifts must be innate, because he is one of those great rarities, a genuinely superior 'chosen one'. He will pass on all his knowledge to me, provided I prove myself worthy of him and behave like a respectful disciple.

There is always a moment during the teachings when my father adopts a very solemn tone. 'Now, listen to me carefully. What I am going to tell you is of utmost importance.' He then explains to me that these occult powers can be misused. Selfish people with despicable intentions might exploit them to appropriate power and wealth. That's what Hitler tried to do, and Nero before him, and Philip the Fair, who persecuted the Knights Templar. These vile sorcerers sully sacred powers and drag the world down into the very depths of chaos. Worse still, they obstruct the work of the Beings of Light, who for millennia have devoted themselves to saving the universe from its fall into the prison of matter.

In order to help me understand the tragedy of this downfall, my father often tells me about one of his former lives, in which he conversed with the spirits on the banks of the Nile: 'The pyramids were under construction. There were no books yet; I read from tablets.' At the time he was Hiram of Tyre, the famous architect who went on to build Solomon's temple with the bronze pillars called Jachin and Boaz on either side of the entrance, symbols of the balance between opposing forces. He describes his tragic fate as the wise Hiram, who is famous among Freemasons the world over. He was betrayed by some craftsmen, to whom he was planning to pass on the 'secret of the masters'. Hiram trusted these men, but because they were vain and impatient, they ambushed him by the door to the temple, and when they failed to extract the 'master word' from him, they stabbed him to death. And so the word was lost forever. My father and his teachers believe this loss is the cause of the world's fall into the darkness of matter.

Hiram's death fills me with despair too: had he not been so shamefully betrayed and assassinated, my father would lead a normal life and I wouldn't have to accomplish this redemptive mission that's so far beyond my abilities. My father genuinely believes that this tragedy will be repeated, that his disciples will want to kill him all over again. But this time he's relying on me to prevent the crime. Thanks to my long years of training, I will be able to distinguish true masters from imposters, to thwart traitors and their plots, and save my father—in other words, Hiram—along with his sacred tenet. That is the reason I am here on earth; that is why he created me. My role is crucial to the entire universe because, by annihilating these traitors, I will at last give the Beings of Light an opportunity to work with perfect serenity in their efforts to free the mind from the cage of matter. Thus, after millennia spent in darkness, everything will be purified and regenerated.

In order to prepare for this titanic undertaking, to restore the universe to its rightful path, I have an enormous amount of work to do on myself. But none of it will be possible if I am not completely dedicated to my mission.

For a start I must cast out the stupid, childish notions that still clutter my mind. No, the world is not a paradise and men are not saints. People betray, steal, kill and readily descend into cannibalism if no one watches over them. 'Love is a colossal sham to amuse the masses. If anyone ever tells you he loves you, don't believe him. It will be because he wants something from you: your power or your money. Never, never, never trust anyone. I alone know what's good for you. If you do as I say, you can rule the world and overthrow the darkness.'

The best position from which to wage this battle would

obviously be as Pope. Unfortunately, I could never have any claim to the role because apparently every future Holy Father has to undergo a trial in which a bishop reaches a hand under the aspirant's robes, feels his testicles and announces loudly in Latin, 'He has testicles, they are indeed there.'

I may not be able to be Pope but I could become the President of the French Republic. There's something even better, though: 'Kings come and go, presidents come and go, but others remain, the Cardinal Mazarins, the Richelieus and the Madame de Pompadours, who are the true wielders of power.' My father tells me that these éminences grises who run the world from behind the scenes are Initiates given specific missions by other Initiates. Madame de Pompadour, a highly cultured woman, gave her support to the Count of Saint-Germain, working alongside him to raise everyone's level of awareness, in order to allow primal energies to circulate. By doing this, they contributed to the advent of the Enlightenment movement, while also facilitating the process of reincarnation of the Beings of Light. Unlike Madame de Pompadour, Mazarin and Richelieu sadly failed: lured by wealth and power, they used their energies 'in the wrong direction' and died of horrible diseases.

Besides Madame de Pompadour, I can draw inspiration from other examples of strong women, such as Joséphine de Beauharnais, a superhuman who was originally at Napoleon's side to guide him. But when success went to his head, he lost touch with Joséphine's beneficial influence, which is what eventually led to his deservedly pitiful demise. In a different mould, Charlotte Corday, who assassinated the radical Jacobin Marat, was an admirable woman who acted for the good of

France and not on a whim, as is often claimed.

Joan of Arc, on the other hand, was only a half-Initiate, lacking knowledge, and that is why she allowed herself to be led astray into idiotic religious devotion instead of lending her support to the Beings of Light. If Joan of Arc had been better educated she could have helped lead the world away from the path of darkness. All the same, the Beings of Light didn't hold that against her: they saved her from being burned at the stake with the help of the Knights Templar and Bishop Cauchon, who is incorrectly depicted as her persecutor. The true story has been obscured, as it often is. Very few people know that Joan went on to marry and live out her days peacefully.

My father has a real passion for one exceptional heroine: Blandina, whose purity pacified the lions that were released to maul her in the arena, although she was then martyred by the Romans. Sadly, she too lacked teachings. If she had had the words to rally the crowds when those lions lay subjugated at her feet, she could have had the Emperor killed, and overthrown the empire... Of course, manipulating a crowd is an extremely difficult art: 'You have to act quickly because if you wait too long, the sheep won't move. And when you succeed in mobilizing them you have to get out of harm's way immediately because they always turn on the powerful and trample them underfoot.'

I emerge from these sessions groggy and dejected. I can see that my father expects me to bring lions to heel, like Blandina, and hold forth in front of troops, like Joan of Arc, and to do it all with the class and subtlety of Madame de Pompadour...How will I ever manage such feats? Worst of all, I'm betraying my father by nurturing a secret longing for an ordinary life.

Ravaillac

Once my father has made up his mind what new outbuildings we are to construct in the grounds over the coming summer—a workshop, an aviary, among other projects—he must reach a decision about where they should be built, which he does with the help of a pendulum. He sits in state on his wooden crate and instructs us to walk around the garden until we reach a spot that inspires him. Then he takes out the pendulum, which he keeps on a velvet cushion in a green case, and dangles it at the end of its string. My mother and I have to stand motionless behind him while the pendulum circles for ages. Finally, my father shakes his head and puts it away. Then the whole performance is repeated for as many times as it takes to find the perfect site.

My father did not consult the pendulum when he decided to build the gymnasium directly over Arthur's grave. This man who has endless theories about the hereafter, about energies, the planets, can't come up with a single explanation for this choice. It's as if he wishes Arthur never existed, as if he wants the creature I loved most in the world to sink into oblivion.

My father is still keen for me to be a potential recruit for a circus. Until the gymnasium is completed I have to do my somersault training in the dining room, and go onto the verandah to practise walking on my hands, handstands and the splits. I have no idea how to do any of these things. Neither do my parents, but they stubbornly continue to instruct me: 'Put your hands on the ground, swing your legs towards the wall and stay like that.' As physical contact is still strictly forbidden, neither of them helps me by holding my legs. Only after countless attempts and dozens of falls do I just about manage to do a headstand.

With somersaults, though, even after months of attempts, I can't get my legs to 'flip over'. My father is infuriated by my repeated failures, and my mother says accusingly, 'If you can't do it, it's because you don't want to. It's a question of willpower.' I keep hurting myself by falling flat on my back. My career in the circus is anything but promising.

My father also wants me to shake off my ridiculous fear of rats. From time to time he comes with me when I go to collect the duck eggs. He stands outside while I go into their shelter, where I often come face to face with a big muskrat ready to attack. I mustn't scream or run away; if I do I risk having to spend the night locked in the duck shed.

Muskrats swarm all around the duck pond. I often spot them swimming through the black water. Sometimes when I do something cowardly I have to go and swim in that pond. Luckily this punishment is rare. I think my mother intervenes because she's the one who would have to fish me out if I got into trouble in the water.

Far from abating, my terror of rats has actually become a full-fledged obsession. My mother and I are responsible for cleaning the zinc gutters on all the outbuildings in the grounds. We put a long ladder up against the wall and take turns going up to clear the rotten leaves that are blocking the drainpipes. One time when I scooped up a disgusting pile of vegetation, I felt something strange. I looked at the bundle in my hands and realized I was holding a dead rat with one of its eyes dangling out of the socket. My legs gave way and I fell, scraping myself badly on the rungs of the ladder. After that, I blacked out completely.

Ever since then, my father need only say, 'Today you'll go and clean the gutters' for me to start feeling nauseous. Meanwhile my mother climbs up blithely and balances at the top of the ladder without holding on to anything. I get vertigo just from watching her.

When a wave of terror washes over me, I experience the physical sensation of my limbs being pulled until they are ripped off, as if I were being subjected to the torture of quartering that my father describes in the story of Ravaillac's death. He tells me that after Ravaillac's limbs were ripped off by four horses, he was left on the ground, to die in agony—it took more than a day. My father opens a book and shows me a terrifying illustration with the caption 'The torture of Ravaillac'. As he talks, I become Ravaillac: no glimmer of hope, my limbs ripped off. It's all over and my only prospect is protracted agony before a gloating crowd.

I'm so paralyzed with fear that I listen only distractedly to the rest. My father claims Ravaillac was the victim of a plot. He did not in fact kill King Henri IV, who was actually killed by one of his own companions who was travelling in the carriage with him. I must get used to the idea that innocence is no protection from an excruciating and unjust death. 'That's true human nature for you, that's what the outside world can do to us, even—or particularly—if we're innocent. Our will and mental strength alone can protect us.'

The quartering feeling that takes hold of me on that ladder is terrible, so much so that my body gradually learns to keep going like a soldier under fire, or rather like an automaton. The life drains out of me, everything is extinguished, inside me there's no life. Once the task is finished I feel none of the relief or pride or satisfaction of a job well done. There is just my deserted body. Only hours later do my senses start to reemerge, but it's a difficult process, as if the life seeping back one drop at a time has been sapped forever of its strength.

I use the same technique to survive the 'meditations on death', which still take place about once a month. The cellars have undergone major building work, but any hope that they would be better is dashed. The new flooring unfortunately only amplifies the sound of the rats scurrying.

In spite of everything, I force myself to concentrate on the Beings of Light who are meant to appear to me in the darkness. I'm a little frightened of meeting my grandmother's spirit, which is often present in the house: my father says she visits him in his bedroom at night. The dead know everything, and I'm afraid she'll tell him that instead of carrying out the exercises he expects of me, I'm completely preoccupied by my fear, obsessed by the sound of the rats, and long for only one thing: the light bulb to come on again.

147

The Brick Wall

In the dangerous world into which my mission will someday take me, I will have to remember the protection that is my birthright as the daughter of a Grand Master of Freemasonry and a great knight of a secret order. If I'm kidnapped or find myself facing a firing squad, there's no need to panic. I just have to remember: to cross my hands, turn them upwards above my head and cry, 'Oh Lord, is there no help for the widow's child!' Help will come. Someone from the firing squad will halt the process and save me. Or a farm labourer working in the fields nearby will draw his weapon and come and set me free. Any ordinary passer-by could turn out to be a Freemason and will do whatever is necessary to help me.

I myself have to carry out a series of preparatory exercises, such as concentrating on my hands in order to make them slimmer and slimmer until they can slip out of handcuffs. Or focusing on the metal of the handcuffs or hemp of the ropes in order to 'move' them. I'm also taught that if I close my eyes I can leave my body to listen to what's being said in the next room. These lessons are still only theory at this stage, because at my age there's a risk that a stronger or more experienced entity could take over my body while I'm 'away', and I would not then be able to return. I have to practise imagining a silver thread connecting me to my bodily vessel so I can find my way back. I must wait until I'm twenty-one, the age of initiation, before embarking on my actual training.

Although I don't really believe there's a danger I'll end up facing a firing squad, the idea of leaving my body makes me break out in a cold sweat. My father hammers into me that fear is the 'indulgence of the weak'. But however hard I try, I am terrified all the time.

For some time now my father has made much of his powers of psychic insight. He can get inside the head of whomever he wants whenever he wants. He doesn't even need to be physically present because he can move about without being seen. I have to understand that I can never hide anything from him: 'I am everywhere. I see everything. Whatever you do, I know about it. Whatever you go on to do, I'll know.' I don't know why he is so insistent. Does he think I am hiding ideas, hatching unholy plans?

Sometimes when I lie in bed at night I feel overwhelmingly sad. I cradle my pillow and imagine someone consoling me affectionately. I say the words I'd like to hear, 'Don't cry, my child. Don't worry, you're not alone. We love you, you know. You're not as bad as you think, you'll come to learn.' But they are soon drowned out by a reprimanding voice: 'Go ahead! Feel sorry for yourself...What a drama queen!'

It's as if someone has flicked a switch: I have an irrepressible urge; I have to punish myself right away. I start by digging my nails into my thighs. But this isn't punishment enough. I bite savagely into my upper arm, knowing no one will see the marks. I drive my teeth deeper and deeper into my flesh and keep my jaws clamped down for longer and longer.

Night after night I inflict abuse on myself, even drawing blood. It's strangely calming. I know the pain will stop whenever I want. I was the one who decided when it should start; I will be the one to decide when it stops. However much it hurts, I draw some comfort from the idea that I'm in control.

I can't take it anymore, I can't put up with this suffering I neither understand nor know when it will end. But when I gradually release my clamped teeth, the loathing and contempt I feel for myself fade correspondingly. The storm of insults raging inside my head eventually abates too and I can finally fall sleep.

I try confusedly to find a way of blocking my father's intolerable intrusions into my thoughts. If he can get inside my head at will, the animals I love are in danger too. If I let Linda out slightly earlier than usual, I have to make sure my father can't 'read' this in my mind because he would take it out on her and I couldn't bear that. So I try to keep my mind blank. I force myself to wipe away any thoughts, or rather not to think of anything, to remain 'absent of thoughts'. As I open the door to her kennel, I keep saying, 'Absent of thoughts, absent of thoughts...' Similarly, when I hide Bibiche—a stray cat who has just had kittens in the garden—I create a sort of blackout inside my head. If my father can find their hideout by delving through my mind, I'm sure he'll take his shotgun and kill Bibiche and her litter.

At times I build a brick wall at the entrance of my head and take shelter behind it to think. The idea came to me when I was helping Albert and Rémi with construction work. I've often watched them build walls and now I know how to do it. You have to concentrate hard and keep an eye on lots of little details: the consistency of the mortar must not be too soft or too dry; there can't be too much or too little on the trowel; the brick must be positioned the right way when you tamp it down; each new layer of bricks has to be level…And before you know it, you have a wall in front of you and you can't see beyond it! In my mind's eye I construct one as I've seen it done: I scoop up some mortar with a trowel, take a red brick and nestle it into place, then more mortar, another brick…I set up a whole row of bricks, then move on to the next and so on. The work goes quickly because my mind builds walls at lightning speed. I just have to think 'brick wall' and there it is in a matter of seconds.

I build my brick wall every now and then, particularly when I want to do something in secret. If my father were to come across the wall he would think he'd bumped into my stupidity. He often tells me that labourers forced to carry out repetitive tasks—like tightening nuts and bolts or working in a production line—end up as morons. That is indeed the best way to dumb down the masses: make them do the same thing over and over, let them have their fireworks every Bastille Day and let them gorge themselves every New Year's Eve. When the body repeats the same action, the mind adopts it and keeps the repetition going day and night, stopping all thought processes. So I persuade myself that, if my father sees my brick wall, he'll think I've been 'contaminated' by my construction work with Albert and Rémi.

My mother is also obsessed with the idea that I hide my thoughts and dress them up in lies. 'If you lie,' she warns me, 'I'll know straightaway because your father will be dead in the morning.' This threat sets my mind racing. Although I sometimes picture myself living happy and free without my parents, I'm terrified at the thought of my father dying and leaving me alone in this sinister world. Anyway, I don't see how or what I could lie about, given how closely I'm monitored. But my mother hounds me so much about the paramount importance of total transparency that a diabolical idea eventually pops into the back of my mind: what if I tried a little lie, really small, a tiny lie, just to see what happens?

I have to say that since the incident with the tiger rug I've had my suspicions. If my father knows everything and sees everything, how come he walked over that tiger rug morning and evening for a week without noticing we had moved it? How come he didn't realize we came within an inch of destroying his sacrosanct bronze Athena?

After much hesitation, I test out a very minor lie relating to a secondary 'rule' concerning toilet paper. When I go pee I'm allowed to use only one square. This itself is a 'favour' I'm granted because in the past women used no paper at all. 'You didn't use more than you're allowed, did you?' My mother often asks and I say no. 'Do you swear you didn't?' she adds. So one day I decide to use two squares of toilet paper.

Everything goes fine until bedtime…then in the night I'm plagued by nightmares. I see a firing squad but it's not me up against the wall, it's Linda or Bibiche—they have to pay for my crimes. Or when I go to wake my father I find him dead. So everything he said is true! I wonder anxiously how he'll be reincarnated. I'm terrified he'll want to be reincarnated into me, expelling me from my own body and taking it over. I finally wake with a start because in the dream, when I open my mouth to speak, it's my father's voice that comes out.

When I go to knock on his door the next morning, I'm full of dread. Eventually I hear 'Come in.' He's not dead, then. He's not even sick. I don't know whether I'm relieved or distressed. Over the next few days I come up with other little lies: I slightly change the itinerary of my early morning walk but claim I've obeyed the instructions; I make small alterations to my solfège exercises; or when I walk past the statue of Athena I spit out 'I hate you' or 'You're ugly', even though I'm supposed to worship her.

Despite my minor infringements and major insults, the threat of imminent death is never fulfilled. A criminal idea gradually insinuates its way into my head: is it possible that my father isn't actually a superhuman with the gift of great powers? Is it possible that everything he says is just hogwash?

The thought is horrifying and exhilarating. All the same, I wonder whether the Beings of Light somewhere in the universe aren't keeping a close tally of all my wrongdoings, and I ask myself whether some day I'll end up torn limb from limb by my own lies: a Ravaillac who, in this instance, fully deserves the torture.

The Grey Vest

In the parcel from the La Redoute catalogue comes my new pair of black shoes with a small one-inch heel; I'll be wearing them for the next year. I try them on and they pinch my feet. My mother ordered them without measuring my feet, simply choosing the next size up from the previous pair. I don't know whether I've grown more quickly than I was supposed to, but these shoes really hurt. When I mention this she tells me, 'It's an issue of willpower.' My father tells me about Chinese women, highly evolved creatures who have their feet bound to keep them small. I should accept how lucky I am and stop complaining. It would be unthinkable to place a special order for me. I can't possibly revert to the previous pair, which is falling apart. The soles have so many holes in them that recently I had been slipping leaves inside them to stop my feet from getting too wet.

I also now have to wear a horrible vest in heavy grey tweed that my father has had specially made for me. He wants me to wear it summer and winter, over my blouse or my jumper. It was made too big for me so that I could keep it for several years, and it has six pockets in which I have to keep a fountain pen, a ballpoint pen, a pencil, a pencil-sharpener, an eraser, a piece of blotting paper, a small notebook, and sheets cut from the letterhead paper of my father's various Masonic organizations. I also have to have a few aluminium clips to hold papers together—not normal paper-clips, which my father thinks are 'accessories for the lazy'—and a box of pen nibs, which must be kept in a separate pocket from the fountain pen. These are specifically for musical scores, which have to be written in pen and ink. I also have a handkerchief, a screwdriver with a bit of cork over its tip so I don't hurt myself on it, and a compass which I must use to escape if I'm kidnapped. If this happens and I have to make my way through a forest, my father advises me always to head north, otherwise I'll end up going around in circles.

An inside pocket is intended for German vocabulary cards— with a word written in German on one side and its French translation on the other—that my father has given me to learn. I also have to have a pair of pliers, but because they're very heavy and make the pocket bulge out of shape, I'm usually exempted from carrying them. 'You must keep your tools on you at all times so you can work anytime, anywhere.' Wherever I am, I have to be able to sit a written impromptu exam, pass a Latin test, et cetera. Meanwhile, I should know how to repair a leak at a moment's notice. In my father's view, this vest corresponds to a sort of rank. He compares it to the work aprons of the 'Companions of the

Tour de France', craftsmen who always have their tools with them. The vest means I can never use the 'lazy excuse' of not having the correct tool for the job.

He insists that I keep this vest on from morning till night, except when I play the accordion. But it feels like a burden, a chain constantly reminding me that I have a mission to accomplish. I make the most of every opportunity to take it off, whether for a couple of minutes when I'm alone in my classroom or for thirty seconds when I go to the bathroom. I don't know why my parents are so fixated on it. 'You haven't taken your vest off, have you?' they ask me several times a day. I look them in the eye and reply, 'No, I've kept it on the whole time,' quaking at the idea that they might find out the truth.

But, like the sword of Damocles hanging over my father's head, my lies go undiscovered. I'm beginning to wonder whether I really need to build brick walls inside my head. I also find it increasingly difficult to resist the urge to explore every nook and cranny of this huge building. Of course, I have to be extremely devious. The times when I can escape the permanent monitoring amount to only a few minutes. As all the rooms are locked, the first thing I have to do is find ingenious ways to work out where each key is hidden.

I now know that my father keeps the key to his bedroom under the doorsill. I make the most of the times when my parents are both on the ground floor to slip silently upstairs, take the key carefully from its hiding place, turn it gingerly in the lock and step into the massive master bedroom. Not wasting a second, I go over to the wardrobes that I've been expressly forbidden to open. I find fencing foils and helmets, and quilted jerkins. I've never seen my father fencing. Are these relics of a previous life? In another cupboard I find six or seven different coloured knight's outfits: tunics with a large cross at the chest, long capes, and swords in sheaths with their bandoliers.

Occasionally I manage to slip into my father's office on the ground floor. I look through the drawers, taking great care not to move anything. I find different letterheads: those for the different Masonic Obediences to which he has belonged, some for his garage, and some for the airfield he ran. I don't know exactly what I'm looking for and anyway I can't stay more than two or three minutes. When I leave I make sure I put the key back exactly as it was.

Over time my objective becomes clear: I now search in the hope of finding 'adoption papers' or any document proving that my parents are not my real parents. At night I tell myself that my real parents are away exploring dangerous parts of the world. They had to entrust me to this rich couple who are now refusing to hand me back. That's why I'm kept prisoner.

My mind often drifts back to the secrets hidden in the two safes in my father's office. I feel that the key to my life is in them. I sometimes wonder what I would do if I could access these documents. I'd need to take them, run away immediately and head straight for the police station. But how to get out of this place? There are bars on the windows, the front door is always locked and, despite all my efforts, I've never worked out where that particular key is hidden. The more I think about it, the less hope I have.

In the build-up to Christmas I promise myself I'll alert the postman or the local firefighters when they come by for their annual tip. I don't know why but my parents prefer to stay out of sight and give me the envelope with the money, which I hand through the small window in the dining room. I realize I could slip a plea for help into the envelope. During the hour I have alone for my homework I try to compose a note. I start ten different versions that all begin with the words 'Tell the police'. But what to put next? I'm not starved, chained, beaten…Who would believe me?

After lessons I go downstairs, discouraged by my powerlessness. On the floor below I can see my father from behind, sitting in the dining room. A tight fist grips my stomach, as it does every time I stand on this landing. I know I have to be extremely careful about the speed of my footsteps and how much noise they make. If he's fallen asleep and my entrance wakes him with a start, he'll accuse me of 'sneaking up on him'. I deliberately make each stair creak. If I'm in any doubt, I silently go back up a few steps and climb down again, pressing my weight onto the ones that make the most noise.

Once in the dining room, I have to sit with my head lowered and not speak or move a muscle until my mother comes in to eat. My father's presence provokes an uncomfortable mixture of fear and revulsion in me. Out of the corner of my eye I can see him slumped in his chair, his back stooped, wearing his horrible worn-out vest, which stinks of sweat and decay. I turn helplessly towards the window overlooking the street, and through the net curtains I manage to make out cars and trucks going up and down the busy road to Saint-Omer. One time I heard my mother say they were heading for England. Oh, if only I could stow away on one of those trucks!

I have a recurring nightmare: I wake to find my room extraordinarily bright, the house flooded with sunlight, and realize it's way beyond our regulation wake-up time. It's strange my parents have let me sleep so late. I go and knock at my mother's door; no one there. Nor at my father's. I hurry to the dining room; it's empty. Did I miss an instruction last night? I go up to the schoolroom, disconcerted not to have my watch on. I open the door... to find my parents lying under the large table by the blackboard. I lean closer: they are definitely dead. My head spins. 'I killed them,' I think. I must have got up in the night and killed them, like in those stories my father relishes telling about sleepwalkers. That's it, it's over. I feel incredible relief. But then the guilt strikes. I'm horrified. I've done the unthinkable. How will I get out of this? I can't seem to feel any grief for them. I have only one thought: I'll go to prison for killing them. Even in death they have me in their clutches. Should I run? But where? Should I leave them here, close the door and carry on living in this place as if nothing has happened? I wake in a sweat, my heart thudding, frantically wondering whether my nightmare has already come true, whether—in a moment of oblivion—I have already killed my parents.

The Crystal Ball

The gymnasium built on top of Arthur's grave is a huge building, with ceilings eight metres high. It has a pommel horse, parallel bars, a beam, rings, a climbing rope, a ladder, et cetera. I'm now meant to become an accomplished gymnast, with no coach other than my mother and, of course, my own willpower. My parents have ordered sports gear for me: black gymnastic slippers and a pair of shorts.

It's the first time I've ever worn shorts. On my way to the gym where my mother is waiting for me to do an hour of exercises, I pass Rémi, who is putting the finishing touches to the outside of the building. He notices something at the back of my thigh. 'What's that big scar?' he asks, looking uncomfortable. 'Oh that? I don't know, I've got another one here,' I say, pointing to my chest. He looks increasingly horrified. A deluge of shame comes crashing down on me. These two scars have always been there, but I've never really thought about them. Doesn't everyone have them?

As soon as I get inside the gym I ask my mother about them. She replies evasively, saying they're marks caused by an X-ray she had when she was pregnant. But Rémi's repulsion pierces me. I feel 'branded', like an animal heading to slaughter. I see myself every day in the large mirror in the gym, and now I can't help noticing the furrow running all along my thigh under the line of my buttock.

I'm haunted by the image of this grimace-like scar. Whenever I'm in the gym I twist and turn in front of the mirror to get a better look at it. Yes, it looks like a big toothless mouth, its lips turned inwards, sown carelessly together with a row of big, uneven stitches. On bath days I try to get a better look at the other scar, which runs around my left side from my chest up under the armpit. It's a swollen, snaking gash, hatched with big sloping hemstitches. When I run my finger over the notches I can feel a tangle of dips and bumps under the hardened skin. I feel mutilated, like Gwynplaine in Victor Hugo's *The Man Who Laughs*. It feels as if, like him, I have 'a cesspit of pain and anger in my heart and a mask of contentment on my face'.

A few weeks later I bring up the subject again with my mother. This time she explains that, shortly after we came to the house, when I was not yet four, I was playing in the garden and fell through the basement window above the cellar, injuring my thigh. When I tried to climb back up, I injured my chest. Has she forgotten about the 'marks caused by the X-ray'? Apparently not, because a few weeks after that she reverts to her first explanation.

161

Later still, she makes a vague reference to an 'initiation'.

I do not dare talk about the scars with my father. I can't imagine asking him even the most trifling question. 'Sneaking up on him' by questioning him when my mother has already given me her answer would smack of betrayal. Besides, he himself sometimes brings up the subject during lessons about the dead, but never in connection with X-rays or a fall: 'You must learn to move between the realms of the living and the dead, as Beings of Light do. Your scars are identifying signs that will help the latter recognize you when you meet between realms.'

I can't really see the connection between identifying signs and scars from a fall as a child. But perhaps my father is using a coded language for some higher level of initiation, and I'll understand only later in my training? I desperately hope that at some stage he'll tell me that these horrible marks will fade away. Ever since Rémi blanched at the sight of my scar I feel even more like a breed apart than before. I don't want to be like the criminals of days gone by, whom my father talks about: branded with an 'L' for forced Labor and an 'F' for Forger. I am not a criminal. Once the Beings of Light have recognized me, there will be no further reason for my scars to exist, and I do hope they disappear.

Luckily my initiation is going ahead in leaps and bounds. Three or four times a year, on precise dates known to my father, he says to my mother, 'Go to your room, Jeannine, and don't come out until I call you.' Then he summons me to the ballroom and I know this means we'll be performing what I call the 'ritual of the crystal ball'. My father never talks about it so I don't know how he would describe this ball, or whether it is actually made of crystal. He puts on white gloves, then takes out a square box made of blond wood from the large bookcase.

We sit down facing each other. He lifts off the lid. Then, holding the wooden base in both hands, he carefully places it onto the table, the ball balancing on its support. It's crucial not to touch it, even with the tips of our fingers, so as not to 'damage its purity'. He makes circular movements with his hands a couple of inches from the surface of the ball. Then it's my turn to take over with these clockwise movements. When he feels we should 'rebalance' the energies, I have to circle my hands the other way.

I don't really understand what all this is for and I think I'd rather not know. Some instinct buried deep inside me is whispering, 'Be careful, if you get involved in this you'll never get away, you'll stay locked up here forever.' But at the same time I'm scared of doing something wrong, because my father puts such emphasis on the correct orientation of energies: 'It's because Hitler reversed the energies of the swastika that everything blew up in his face.'

Then he takes out one of his pendulums. He has dozens of them, but the green one, with the green string and the green case, is his favourite. While he rotates it around the ball to 'recharge it with energy' I barely breathe, feeling as if something portentous is happening right before my eyes. Next he goes to sit further away, leaving me alone, looking at the ball. I have to stare right at it and 'open myself up to its teaching'.

Once, while I'm concentrating on the ball, all of a sudden I hear snoring. After a quick glance to check that he really is asleep, I decide to give free rein to my devilish curiosity. This ball is such a mystery! Is it even crystal? I need to touch it. I bring my hands slowly closer; my breathing accelerates. If I touch it, will everything explode? But I can't fight the urge; I have to know. Even so, I give a little start when my hands come into contact with it. Nothing happens. My fingers don't disappear. I'm fascinated by the strange substance. It's not glass; it's dense and opaque. I lift it up a little. I'm so surprised by the weight of it that I lurch to one side and almost drop it. Fear slams through me and my hands start to shake under the weight of the ball. Luckily my father carries on snoring. Still holding the ball, I manage to get to my feet without scraping my chair. Now I'm standing holding the ball firmly in both hands and I try to put it back on its stand. For some minutes I struggle to position the ball so that it remains stable. Then by some miracle, I find the correct angle and it slips perfectly into place.

When I sit back down the screech of my chair wakes my father. He gives a little cough and comes to sit opposite me. I stay motionless, as if under a spell, my eyes glued to the ball. He must notice the sweat on my face, the mistiness in my eyes and the moistness under my nose, because I can hear the satisfaction in his voice as he says, 'Aha, there we are! You're finally opening up to it...'

To my horror I suddenly notice my fingerprints on the ball. I'm going to be incinerated on the spot, either by the ball itself or by my father's anger. 'That's enough for today,' he says, taking the base in his gloved hands. He does a sort of bow before putting the thing back in its box. I stammer something about not feeling very well and run to the bathroom to throw up.

When I come out of the bathroom I'm startled to find him standing guard by the door. Oh God! The ball has given away my crime! He eyes me probingly. 'That's good, you're starting to understand and accept the teaching.' I mutter that I need to go back to the bathroom. To my surprise he accepts this. I hear his voice through the door: 'The pollutants in your mind and body are being expelled. This is what knowledge will do for you.'

At night I sometimes wonder whether I should go down with a cloth and wipe off my fingerprints. But I never find the courage to do it. So my stomach liquefies every time my father summons me to the ballroom. I picture him opening the box and the ball squealing, 'She touched me!' Or my father eventually noticing the fingerprints. In my fear I swallow hard and produce great beads of sweat. Meanwhile my father is still convinced I'm opening my mind to the knowledge of the Initiates. Luckily, my mother is excluded from this initiation. She would notice the unholy marks straightaway.

Périsaut

After two years of painful, clumsy attempts, I finally manage to execute three somersaults three days in a row. My father rewards me by buying me a pony that he baptizes 'Périsaut'. Arthur died two years ago; I miss him. A new pony won't bring my friend back. But my father doesn't understand that.

When Périsaut arrives, the big gates are opened for the delivery truck. The seller leads out a small animal whose coat is brown and beige—it looks like a dog. Périsaut is a Shetland pony only a few months old. 'You must wait until he's at least six months old before riding him or you could break his back,' the man warns.

My father has come up with a whole training program. Périsaut will help out with trimming the grass: he is tied to a big iron stake in the middle of the lawn from eight in the morning until eight in the evening. Now, my father explains, he'll create 'perfect circles' as he grazes around this central point. I go to fetch him from his stable and my mother attaches the metal chain to his collar. But nothing goes as planned: the pony is so tiny that the weight of the chain makes him tip forwards onto his knees. We have to accept that the chain needs to be replaced with a rope, but Périsaut regularly chews through it and goes wandering around the grounds.

Although he doesn't openly admit it, my father abandons his plans for circular grazing and instead sets about training Périsaut in order to show me how psychological conditioning works. A few months earlier I had to mark out a three-metre-diameter circle in the levelled-area of the garden. This was where my father wanted me to work on my somersaults. He now wants to make Périsaut stay inside this circle. He tells me to fetch one end of an electric fence and hold the pony firmly by the collar. Every time Périsaut sets a hoof on the white line I have to give him an electric shock in the chest. My mother stands guard on the other side of the circle with a riding whip, which she cracks along his back if he tries to step out. Périsaut is terrified; he rears and whinnies. He kicks me several times and gives me a huge bite on the arm. I still have the scar. While I'm forced to torture him, I silently ask his forgiveness.

Eventually Périsaut gives in. Now when I take him into the circle he lowers his head and stays there, making no attempt to leave. In the evenings my father summons me to his room and turns on the outside light in that levelled area to point out that the conditioning is working. It's often raining and I watch the water running down poor Périsaut's mane as he stands in his circle.

During these training ordeals, all I'm allowed to bring him is water. I whisper to him that, although he and I don't understand these exercises, there may be some valid reason for them that we can't see. Périsaut gazes at me with sad eyes that seem to ask: 'Why?'

His *why*s amplify all the *why*s that have obsessed me for so long. Why should Linda be shut in? Why must Périsaut be tied up? Why am I not allowed out? Why must I not derive any pleasure from eating? Why does Yves stub out his cigarettes on my knee? Why does Raymond do what he does to me? Why can't I have any heating in my bedroom? Why don't we wash? Why does no one kiss and hug me like people do in books? Why am I not allowed to go to school with other children? Why?

But the biggest why is: why does my mother hate me so much? Yesterday I showed her where my eyelid was swollen from a spider bite. I looked at myself in the mirror and said, 'I look like a monster.'

'If that's how you see yourself,' she replied icily, 'then that's the real you: a monster on the inside.'

Menie Grégoire

My compulsory reading continues with an author whom I instantly dislike: Sade. My father, who always refers to him as the 'Marquis de Sade', talks of him in rapturous terms: 'Now, there's a man who really got it. He was never fooled by sheep or manipulators! And that's why he ended up imprisoned...' He occasionally takes out one of Sade's books, chooses a long passage—usually on a philosophical topic—and uses pieces of blotting paper to mark the beginning and end of the extract. Then he tells me to sit alone in the ballroom and read it. I loathe reading Sade: it chills me to the bone and all I want to do is finish so I can go and knock three times on the dining-room door for my father to come and put the book away.

My father wants to get rid of the 'dimwit' in me; it exasperates him and he's relying on Sade's sound ideas to help him. If I happen to show my enthusiasm for the characters in, say, *The Odyssey*, he replies, 'Stop believing what others want you to believe. Penelope was never faithful, she bedded all her suitors. No woman is ever faithful. As for Telemachus, he was homosexual. And if Ulysses' dog wagged his tail when he saw his master, it's only because he hoped he'd throw him a bone.'

I nod in agreement. But Edmond Dantès, Gavroche, Rodolphe, Man Friday, Ulysses and Telemachus are still the heroes I adore. I talk to them inside my head, and they reply. I listen to Telemachus's tales of his travels with his father. I wish I too had a father who took me on adventures, who could run, jump...

I sometimes also talk to Nancy, whom I met in the Nancy Drew detective series. But our conversations never last long. It's as if there is no common ground between her world and mine. I feel ashamed of myself and of my miserable reclusive life when Nancy is so beautiful, with her immaculate hair, all her friends and a father who loves her.

The conversations with my 'invisible friends' started when I was very young. The first person who visited me was Athena. Not my father's Athena holding the sphere of knowledge at the foot of the stairs, but the one from *The Odyssey*: I adore her because she's intelligent and beautiful. She calms me down when I start to panic. When I'm daunted by the next day's schedule she gives me sound advice. If, for example, I have to go out into the grounds at night and I'm having terrible trouble finding the light switch near the duck pond, I hear her whisper in my ear: 'Count your footsteps so you don't get lost. You know it's twenty-eight paces to the right before you reach the switch...'

I've never mentioned this to my parents. I'm sure my father

wouldn't like me talking freely with anyone else. Ever since I read Dostoyevsky's *Notes from Underground*, I'm feeling more confident about my mental health. In that book, the hero holds forth to absent listeners for pages on end, and yet he isn't mad. He's mean, which is different.

Sometimes I also invent an older brother who reassures me when I hear strange noises in the house and worry that a ghost is suddenly going to appear in front of me. 'Nothing bad is going to happen to you,' he says. 'I'm here.' I also have schoolfriends and we whisper together on our way downstairs, gossiping about the headmaster, the strict 'Monsieur Didier', who will punish us if we make too much noise, and about our teacher 'Madame Jeannine', who is bound to tell on us. We giggle among ourselves even though we're scared.

But it's when I listen to the radio in secret and hear those glorious voices buzzing with life that I'm most moved. My mother has managed to evade my father's prying eyes and acquire a small transistor radio that she takes to her room every night to listen to her favourite program. She hides it in the classroom during the day because, although my father could decide to search our bedrooms at any time, for some mysterious reason he never searches the classroom. She leaves me alone in the afternoons more and more frequently, so I get through my homework and then, during whatever time I have left, I listen to the radio. She doesn't suspect a thing.

By chance I stumble upon Menie Grégoire's program, in which listeners call in to tell stories about their lives. I'm completely transfixed. To me, she has the most beautiful voice in the world and in a flash it transports me out of the house and beyond my father's reach. What I love most is when Menie says, 'I'm not judgmental.' She seems both very kind and very firm in her views. The people who write to her are like me: they're frightened, they feel stupid, ugly, unloved. And Menie 'understands' them, never condemning them as cowardly or weak. She gives them simple, sensible advice. She even seems to care for them. For the first time in my life I dare to hope that somewhere in the world there might be someone who, though they wouldn't go so far as to love me, might not think me stupid or hate me. Menie is the great Athena, but with added warmth.

Coming back to my father's world afterwards is painfully hard. At the moment Périsaut is the subject of a variety of culinary and alcohol-related experiments. As he is stubbornly refusing to take on his role as a lawnmower, my father has decided the pony should forsake his instincts and become an omnivore. He wants to prove to me that nature itself can't resist his power. Périsaut gets used to eating the same food as us and develops a taste for omelettes. His favourite dish, though, is the same as mine: spaghetti with tomato sauce.

One day my father has some horse meat delivered by the Killer and tells my mother to cook it. Then we are solemnly summoned to witness a crucially important scientific experiment. He fills a tin plate with the meat and adds some tomato sauce. Périsaut eats it all up greedily and my father turns to me triumphantly: 'You see what living beings are like? You think Périsaut is so sweet and affectionate towards you, but he wouldn't think twice about eating you if he could—he's happy enough eating his own kind! People are the same, they're cannibals, quite prepared to betray you and eat you. Do you see now why you can't trust anyone but me?'

I tell him, 'Yes, yes, I understand.' But no, I don't understand why he's so happy to have made a cannibal of Périsaut. When he describes how his own father tricked him into eating his beloved pet rabbit, he gets very emotional. It's as if he's now trying to outwit that cruel man.

Périsaut also has to drink alcohol every day and tackle the white line test like me. He quickly gets used to drinking white wine, red wine, diluted Ricard and mulled wine, but flatly refuses neat Ricard. When he tries to avoid it, three of us have to hold him—my mother, Raymond and me—so that we can pour the alcohol down his throat. As soon as we release him, he lets out the most heart-rending squeals. He never succeeds in walking straight along the white lines and very often falls forwards onto his nose. My father is extremely disappointed.

Périsaut also disappoints my mother by absolutely refusing to let anyone ride him. Despite a storm of whipping, it's impossible to get a saddle on him. He nips at my mother, or bites my father's pants—in short, they can't do anything with him. Eventually they give up.

Hungarian Rhapsody

For three years now, since I was seven, Yves has been my music teacher; for three years he has mistreated me several times a week. He is always beside himself when he's short of money. And he always seems to need money; he is constantly in debt and pursued by bailiffs. My father offers him and his wife Mireille a room on the second floor in exchange for eight hours of music lessons a day, except of course when he's performing at local dances. So Yves moves into our house for a few months. It's a nightmare. I almost end up loathing music.

My schedule is turned upside down to accommodate his availability. When he goes off on tour I can breathe easy for a few days. But the moment he's back I'm in hell all over again. It's as if he's taking out his revenge on me for the extra work imposed by my father. When I play the piano he grabs my hair and yanks my head back, yelling, 'What did I just tell you?' He sometimes makes me stand for more than an hour playing the horrible accordion, which weighs over twelve kilos.

For eight hours a day we alternate between the piano, the accordion, the clarinet, the saxophone and the trumpet. There is also a twelve-stringed guitar, a guitar so huge I can't even get my fingers around the fret-board. On top of all this, my father makes use of the fact that Yves is here to get me started on drums and the pedal organ, both of which he commissions Yves to buy.

I'm fascinated by the organ's double keyboard. Thanks to my familiarity with the piano and the solfège work that Madame Descombes assigned to me, I have a certain facility for reading three-part scores. I decipher Bach's Cantata 147 with relative ease. Yves is amazed and asks whether I've already studied the piece. 'No, but I drew on what Madame Descombes taught me.' He spots the gleam of reverence in my eyes when I mention her, and flies into a temper, tossing the musical scores on the piano across the room. When I see my precious *Hungarian Rhapsody* on the floor, my breath catches. He notices immediately and, with a spiteful look, he grabs it and tears it into tiny pieces.

Liszt's *Hungarian Rhapsody No. 2* is a sacred memento for me. Madame Descombes gave it to me a long time ago with the words, 'This is what you're working towards. One day we'll work on it together.' When I'm sad, I need only think of this score and I have the heart to carry on, as if it were telling me that another life is possible and I'm not condemned to stay here forever.

I don't know why I think of turning to Mireille, Yves's wife. She isn't actually allowed to talk to me and risks being beaten by her irascible husband. All the same I slip her a little note asking her for some sticky tape. There isn't any in the house. But Yves has some, I've seen him use it to stick his scores together. Mireille manages to sneak me a roll of tape. Her kindness makes my heart swell. Still anxious, though, I ask her not to mention this to anyone. She puts a finger to her lips and whispers, 'Don't worry, I know.' That night I stick my precious *Rhapsody* back together one tiny piece at a time, like a jigsaw puzzle. When it's finished I hide it inside my big book of Czerny exercises. Yves loathes that book, so there is little risk of him opening it.

I'm now ten years old and I dare to do things that only a few months ago I would never have dreamt I could do. At night, for example, even though I'm still not allowed to leave my bedroom, I get up and go for 'walks' around the house. They're not walks for the fun of it: I get bruises from bumping into walls, but I hope I'm also inflicting a few bruises on this damned house. I hate the place and I want it to know how I feel.

I do much worse than this. When it's not too cold at night I open my shutters, taking great care not to make them creak. I climb out the window and jump down onto the roof of the verandah. From there I can slide onto the roof of the kennel and land in the garden. After all these years of my father making me walk around the garden at night, I can find my way in the dark without any trouble. Although I still feel a little scared, this is soon outweighed by the thrill of being free. Linda runs to greet me and together we go to find Périsaut, who sleeps standing up over by the henhouse. He usually avoids the stable because he's so afraid of being shut in. But when he sees us on one of these nocturnal trips, he heads over to the stable of his own accord and lies down on the straw. Linda and I nestle against his belly for a few minutes of unadulterated happiness.

I worry about Périsaut's frequent punishments for refusing to drink neat Ricard, or for biting Raymond: he gets locked up between the outside door to the stables and the green gate on the inside. I hate this narrow space; it's exactly where Raymond stands waiting when he wants to catch me. Périsaut stays trapped there in the dark, sometimes for three days in a row.

My father still insists the pony should 'mow' the grass in various places, particularly in front of the bench near the verandah. If he doesn't graze these areas, he earns further punishments. Before climbing back up to my room I make a detour to the lawn and clip the grass around the bench, one clump at a time, using scissors from the stables. My father scrutinizes the grass every day and seems satisfied. He believes his conditioning is working: Périsaut is omnivorous and is less and less keen on eating grass, except in the places where my father wants it cut.

Aspro

Yves and Mireille take all their meals in their room on the second floor. They are very discreet and avoid being in the same rooms as us. But in the evenings we sometimes hear them bickering behind closed doors. Yves is probably no kinder to his wife than to me. Some mornings Mireille comes down with a black eye and a defeated expression.

She's a kind woman, a little chubby, heavily made up, a hairdresser by trade. I'm intrigued by her dark brown hair. I'd love to have pretty, medium-length hair like hers, like the girls in the La Redoute catalogue. My father has always forbidden both my mother and me from wearing our hair even half an inch shorter. 'Whores have short hair, which is why during the war…' His reasoning leaves us perplexed. Meanwhile, we have hair down to our waists. We're even instructed to touch it as little as possible, and to wash it only once a month. My mother always wears hers up, and mine is always braided because 'loose hair over the shoulders is for women of loose morals'. As for our foreheads, they have to be kept clear to 'allow the free circulation of intelligence'. According to him, 'a pair of curtains in front of the eyes keeps stupidity inside'.

After my German lesson one day, I summon all my courage and make a sacrilegious request: I ask my father whether he would allow Mireille to cut my hair a little. He glowers at me. 'Do you really want this? All right,' he says simply. Days go by and I daren't remind him that he has given permission. Then, when he comes across Mireille in the corridor, he calls to her, 'Do you have a moment?' She pales visibly. I think she is more afraid of him than I am. 'Do you have your hairdressing things? Go and get them. You're going to take care of Maude.' She relaxes. 'Oh yes, I'd be delighted. But I'll have to wash her hair first—'

'No need,' he interrupts.

She comes back down with her bag.

'Shave her head,' my father snaps.

She freezes for a moment, then says in a wavering voice, 'I could give her a pretty little short haircut…'

'Shave her head.'

While she runs the clippers over my scalp, I can read the heartbreak on her face in the mirror. My long blonde hair falls like the strips of hemp we bind around the water pipes in winter to stop them freezing. I avoid looking at myself, ashamed. And yet I didn't sleep with the Germans. If my father is subjecting me to the same punishment as those unworthy women he sometimes describes, then I must be truly worthless. Perhaps I'm being punished for the humiliating experiences I undergo with Raymond…

I wait for her to finish. I look up and turn to stone. I don't recognize my own face, which is even uglier than before. Clearly visible on my scalp are dozens of little scars I inflicted on myself as a child, when I banged my head against walls. Over the next few weeks my head itches. I feel more and more of a stranger in my own body, and avoid mirrors even more than before. My parents must be pleased because they can't stand me looking in the mirror. If my father catches me glancing in a mirror, he makes his voice sound nasal and snidely sings *Avez-vous vu le nouveau chapeau de Zozo*[1]*?* I'm filled with shame. Mireille avoids me now, as if she can't bear the guilt of my bare scalp.

The new hair growing back is not so blonde. It's now light brown, which seems to cause my parents great consternation. Whenever my father mentions Blandina he makes much of her luminous hair and glances disapprovingly at my head. Initiated women are very fair. As a child, my mother had hair so fair it was almost white, and I get the feeling that was why my father chose her as my future mother. I was extremely blonde too, but none of that matters now.

When my hair grows back I slash aggressively at the locks that fall over my face, so that they now look like a sort of demented staircase. I cut randomly into their thick mass, leaving gaps on the side or the top. I almost take pleasure in disfiguring myself. As for my eyebrows, which darkened long ago, I rip them out with a small pair of pliers that I steal from the cellar and hide under a

---

1 *Have you seen Zozo's new hat?* This is the first line from the Maurice Chevalier song, *'Le Chapeau de Zozo'*.

carpet bar on the second floor. My eyes now look like an owl's. As ugly goes, you can't get uglier. My father doesn't seem to notice anything. My mother, on the other hand, is triumphant: this is proof that I'm crazy!

Once again my father tells me to go and help Raymond. I go down into the tool cellar and he appears right behind me. I'm trapped. A piece of me dies every time. All at once I hear the door to the other part of the cellar open. Raymond is panting like a dog and doesn't hear a thing. At last something is going to happen to bring an end to this nightmare! I recognize my mother's footsteps. I'm saved: she will finally know what I'm going through. And it will all be over for him. Here she is…She sees me, our eyes meet, and…she looks away. She seems to abandon her plan to do whatever she came down here for, and walks away.

Only a few seconds have elapsed since I heard that door open. I fall into the very depths of despair. She can't have failed to notice Raymond pressed up behind me with his arm clasping my waist. She must have seen my distress…Am I so evil, then, that I don't even deserve a little help?

Winter is coming. My father is still just as afraid of snipers, and is adamant about lowering the mechanical shutters on all the windows overlooking the street before switching on any lights in the evening. For some time now I've been responsible for turning the stiff old crank handles to do this. He sometimes watches anxiously while I grind them around and around. Then one day he decrees, 'From now until the spring we'll keep the shutters closed.' My heart sinks at the thought of spending the winter in these icy rooms that will now be plunged in darkness.

My mind endlessly replays that look we exchanged in the cellar. She saw me, and she looked away...Did she see me? How could she walk away and leave me in the clutches of that filthy vampire? Or did I dream it?

In the mornings we attend to my father's wake-up routine in the dismal half-light. I'm afraid I'll drop the smooth bowl containing his urine. I'm filled with disgust for him, for myself, for this house and the whole world. When I go to empty the pot in the toilet I sometimes feel so sick that I walk too quickly and spill some on my feet. I stand there horrified. I don't have another pair of pants or shoes to change into. My clothes will reek of this hideous smell; it will cling to my skin and brand me forever. I feel sick all the time now.

It's still only September but the temperature is already dropping. I still have to do my thirty minutes of swimming three times a week until October. I dive into the black water as if throwing myself into an abyss. It will be cold forever. Sometimes I think all it would take is to stay underwater and stop breathing...

The days go by, dull and grey. My innate joy has ebbed away once and for all. Whatever I do, tomorrow will be the same, or worse. Only my reading allows me to escape, but the moment I close a book, my oppressive life grabs me by the throat again. When I read Victor Hugo's *Ruy Blas* I feel I'm being killed by the poison he takes. And I die alongside Romeo when he drains the fatal vial. I want to get out of here, and dying would be one way to escape. But how to go about poisoning myself? Where can I find a vial of deadly potion?

For want of poison, I fall back on Aspro, the only medicine in the house. The stock is kept in a drawer in the guest bedroom. I manage to get in there one day on my way back down from the schoolroom, and happen to grab an almost full box. I've made up my mind: today is the day.

In the evening I take the box out from where I've hidden it under my mattress. I can't postpone this as my mother sometimes inspects my bed. But I didn't think of bringing up some water. All the same, I swallow a couple of tablets. But the third gets stuck. I'll have to put off my escape until tomorrow. I hide the box near the fireplace. The next day I have trouble finding a receptacle. I manage to hide a pot of pencils under my vest and fill it with water from the bathroom tap before going back to my room.

Instead of reading, I take the tablets one by one, using the water sparingly. I go to bed and picture my parents finding me comatose, calling for help and taking me to the hospital. They're worried, they take care of me, I'm saved and tomorrow isn't anything like today. But another image immediately overwhelms my mind: my parents are furious, they leave me to suffer, I'm in agony for what seems an eternity. In the end I recover without any intervention, and my teachings become even tougher! No, tomorrow won't be like today, it will be even worse. I get back up and hide the pink packaging under the carpet: if they don't know what I've taken, I'll have a better chance of dying.

I expect to slip gently into oblivion, but my mind starts to fight, as it does in my 'alcohol and will' training. One part of me is ready to let go but the other part braces itself as it considers the consequences: what if Linda stays locked up, what if no one ever lets her out again and she dies having lost her mind? Who will feed Bibiche and her kittens? All night I flit between nightmares, some sleeping some waking. At 6 a.m. I open my eyes. I'm still here, the day is starting again, the same as ever. I feel a little weird, and think maybe that means I'll die later. But evening comes, and I collapse exhausted. Can't even die properly.

Nietzsche

When my correspondence courses contradict my father's teaching, my mother 'sets the record straight'. For example, the history manual describes Vercingetorix as a brave warrior and a talented military leader who stood up to the Roman legions. But my mother announces flatly: 'In reality he was just a prize idiot.' If I point out that in my manual Joan of Arc dies at the stake, when my father says she was saved by the Knights Templar, she says, 'Don't waste time on that. Anyway, it doesn't make any difference now.'

Despite the tight restrictions on my reading, my mind is filling with ideas, some of which my father would find unacceptable. 'You mustn't behave like sheep do,' he says emphatically, 'and believe things just because you've been told them.' On the other hand, I have to accept blindly everything he teaches me, starting with his religious ideas: 'Let's take God and the devil, whom most people consider to be opposites: they are in fact one and the same thing because they are both emanations of the Great Architect of the Universe.' The notion of a 'benevolent God' was engineered by the Church to 'tame people's minds', he tells me. Meanwhile, the notion of the devil was deliberately 'diabolized' to repress creativity. For example, the Inquisition used this concept to persecute great thinkers who were looking for different answers to the fundamental questions. By doing this, it set back humanity's progress.

The world is actually the work of the Great Architect of the Universe. Lucifer, who emanates from him, was the master of light, but he strayed from his path. You have to be wary of what people say about Lucifer. Only the Great Initiates can recognize his hand in certain acts, such as the temptation to turn energies the wrong way.

As for Jesus, he certainly did exist: he was a good man, an Initiate, but not the son of God. Idiot men put him on a cross, but I mustn't take all those stories about crucifixion at face value. My father explains at length that if you put an eighty-kilo man on a cross with a couple of nails through the palms of his hands, his hands would tear and he would fall flat on his face. It couldn't have happened like that. In fact, Jesus ended up tied to his cross with rope. Similarly, Mary was a good woman, but she was definitely no virgin! As sheep are incapable of grasping the significance of a profound message, the Church gives them sensationalism; it's all they're interested in.

And as for Adam and Eve, the angels and the saints—with the exception of a rare few Initiates such as Blandina—they're mostly stories to keep foolish minds occupied. You need only look at Lourdes, 'a perfect example of a sanctuary for stupidity, built to rob suckers of their money and line the Church's pockets...'

That said, there are some good things about the Church. Let's take cathedrals. They were built on 'energy sites', by builders who inherited ancient traditions that go back to the architect Hiram of Tyre, who built the perfect temple in Jerusalem to welcome the Queen of Sheba. As his present-day reincarnation, my father knows what he's talking about. Long ago, cathedrals were initiation sites. If the Initiated proved unworthy of their teaching, stones could come tumbling down upon them. Cathedrals were also sacred places where the poor and unfortunate could shelter from the injustices of the world.

But the problem with the Church is that it cannot tolerate the existence of Initiates independent of its power. Look at the history of the Cathars, true Bringers of Light who were exterminated by the moronic Catholics. As Initiates, the Cathars can be reincarnated. From one life to the next they perfect themselves and accumulate valuable learning. The Church was obviously afraid of their power, but it did not succeed in eradicating them. Their order survived by going into hiding.

The same goes for the order of Templars. They are all superhumans. Their whole organization is based on secrecy, which is why they have not in fact been eliminated as history books claim. They have simply gone into hiding, and they still exist and operate discreetly. My father himself is proof of that. If I follow his teaching diligently, I too will become a Templar and will gain access to the secrets of the universe.

When my father talks about these Beings of Light, he insists

I keep my eyes fixed on his, not even blinking. Deep inside me, an alarm goes off, and I secretly resist what he's saying. But a part of me can't help listening to these strange and wonderful stories. Like the story of Noah, a truly great Initiate whom the Bible misrepresents. Noah was in fact a clairvoyant who could recognize Beings of Light, both human and animal. He brought them together in the Ark, knowing that all creation was going to be abolished because it had been corrupted by the insatiable pursuit of material wealth. Noah sacrificed himself: like my father, he withdrew from the world to watch over his protégés, so that life on earth could start over after the flood.

Deep down I'm fascinated by Noah. I'm fascinated by Isis, the widow of Osiris and mother of all Freemasons. I'm sometimes summoned to the billiard room to learn about Hermes Trismegistus. 'Hermes Three-Times-Great,' my father calls him. A little voice inside me thinks cynically, 'There's the number three again.' But I'm actually dazzled by the large book he has open in front of me. At the bottom of the title page I see: 'Didier & Co., booksellers and publishers.' So my father wrote this magnificent book! I have to read a number of rather obscure passages, and stroke particular pages, making a circular clockwise movement three times (there it is again!). His deep voice gets right inside my head, telling me that in this book are the keys to true wisdom. To great alchemy. To understanding the universe. The knowledge held in these pages will pass into my brain. I must receive it; I must open my mind.

I leave these sessions disturbed and anxious. Then my father makes me recite the secret codes that will help me recognize Masons later in life: if I hear someone say 'It's raining,' I have to reply, 'I can't read or write, I can only spell, give me the first letter and I'll give you the second.' If someone shakes my hand in a particular way, I have to say, 'I'm seven years old.' I find this apprenticeship exciting: it means I'll get out some day, and meet other people. Mostly Initiates, but they're better than nothing.

I'm assigned to read Nietzsche's *Beyond Good and Evil*. He's an important philosopher and my father is convinced he will 'help me surpass myself'. I liked *Thus Spoke Zarathustra*, which I read when I was nine. I was astonished by the words 'God is dead', and enchanted by the conversations with animals. I didn't always grasp the meaning of the sentences but enjoyed the way they sounded: 'I love mankind', for example. Nietzsche often writes 'I love'. This word, which is never ever used in our house, seeps into my mind like warm honey. Even the word 'superhuman' doesn't have the same hard, harsh sound to it in Zarathustra's mouth as it does in my father's.

I'm glad I have another book by Nietzsche to read. I tell myself I'll understand it better this time. But I don't at all. My father thinks I've grasped the meaning perfectly. He tells me the story of Nathan Leopold and Richard Loeb, two young Americans fascinated by the concept of a superhuman who has such control over his emotions that he can commit the perfect crime. Leopold and Loeb wanted to prove their own superiority by killing a fourteen-year-old boy. But the crime was far from perfect, because one of them was weak. They were soon arrested and the whole world was fascinated by their trial. My father talks admiringly of Leopold, 'a true disciple of Nietzsche', who saw the murder as an act full of meaning that would allow him to become superhuman. On the other hand, he feels only contempt for Loeb, 'a follower' and therefore 'a monster'. The proof of this is that Leopold changed and developed over the years he was in prison, and now lives free and continues to strive towards the light, whereas Loeb was killed in prison.

I don't really understand the message. Is my father warning me against wanting to prove my superiority by committing the perfect crime? Or is he actually suggesting I should commit one? These questions torment me. When I wake with a start after dreaming yet again that my parents' bodies are under the table in the schoolroom, I find it even harder to shake off my terror. For a few seconds, I have a horrible conviction that I've killed them myself...As part of my initiation...As part of becoming a superhuman.

Mathilde

My meditations on death still happen once a month. I have to remain motionless so that the dead agree to pass into me. They enter by one side, deposit their teachings and leave by the other. Being 'pure', I will naturally absorb only the 'clarity' of their teachings.

My father brings up the subject of my horrible scars again: he finds them useful; thanks to them he would recognize me anywhere. Because I'm 'marked on both sides', whenever he or one of the Chosen Spirits who taught him passes into me, they will know instantly who I am, and feel safe. These spirits have to be extremely vigilant and avoid passing through seemingly pure individuals, who are in fact diabolical decoys, carefully developed by 'master hunters'. The Chosen Spirits risk being trapped inside these 'demon' decoys, who would then be able to siphon out all their knowledge. This would be catastrophic for the survival of the universe.

I don't know if I prefer to know the reason why I have to be tormented in the cellar or not to know. These spirits terrify me almost as much as the rats. I don't want masters passing through me, even Chosen ones. I feel sad for my father, who goes to great lengths to inculcate such an unworthy 'Chosen' subject with his precious knowledge. At the same time, I secretly resent him for thrusting me, gasping, into this sea of terror. When I fall asleep all sorts of spirits—good and evil, light and dark—seethe inside my head. I find it incredibly hard to shut out the sound of my father's voice. In the middle of the night the wall opens softly behind my pillow. Two hands come out, clasp my head and start pulling me backwards. I fight and try to scream but no sound comes out of my mouth. I'm drawn into the wall and it closes around me—I'm walled in alive and no one knows I'm there.

This new nightmare recurs so frequently that I'm afraid of falling asleep. I try to change things by lying with my head at the foot of the bed. There's quite a lot of space between the end of the bed and the chimney. But now it's the fireplace that opens up and the spirits' hands emerge, reach for me and take hold of my head. They pull me towards the chimney, and slide me up inside it. I end up in a hidden cell that no one knows exists.

I can't stand it any longer. If only I could will myself dead. If only my mind could take me far away from this place that I loathe, and take Linda with me. I need to train my mental powers, not to become master of the world, but to help us escape. I make use of my father's exercises: I focus every ounce of my will as if compressing my brain. I close my eyes tight, imagine my scars opening up and all of me pouring out through them. I become a fluid body which flows into the kennel, carries Linda along with it…and together we wake up somewhere else.

Other times I burrow right inside myself, deeper and deeper, as if I were inside a mountain of ice. My vital functions slow. My father has told me that some prisoners managed to escape from concentration camps by doing this. They slowed their heart rate so dramatically that they were presumed dead, loaded onto carts with other corpses and thrown into a mass grave. Once there, they reheated their bodies by imagining they were over a fire. They came back to life and ran away. So I'm training myself to make my heartbeat more and more faint, but I haven't yet worked out how to take Linda with me.

I can't stand mealtimes anymore. I've had enough of being made to eat everything. Enough of being forced to swallow the steak my mother cooks until it's hard as shoe leather, served swimming in burnt butter. With eyes like daggers, my father says, 'Eat it all, you have less than a minute to finish.' Furious, I stuff the whole steak in my mouth. It won't go down. I'm choking, help, I can't breathe. My throat is blocked. I'm going to suffocate…He doesn't move. In the end I put my fingers into my mouth, do my best to grab the piece of meat blocking my throat, and eventually manage to fish it out onto my plate. My head is spinning. 'Pick that up and go and put it in the toilet,' my father says.

I have had enough of swallowing everything like a machine. Enough of suffocating and retching under my father's contemptuous eye. There's a fight every Friday, the day my mother serves another dish I loathe: fish in mustard sauce. For years I've repressed my nausea, but now I refuse. I don't say anything but sit there with my arms crossed. Lunch comes to an end and my mother clears the table. My father says his usual, 'You won't get down from the table until you've eaten everything.' He stays sitting opposite, glowering at me. Resolute, I keep my head lowered. Hours go by. A gnawing rage inside me has turned me to stone. In the end he gets to his feet, saying, 'Don't move.' Fine, I won't move. Suppertime comes. They eat in front of me, pretending not to see me. I couldn't care less; all I'm thinking about is how badly I need to use the bathroom. They go up to bed, and I have to help with my father's bedtime routine. This must be the only time I've ever been happy to empty that chamber pot, and I use the opportunity to go to the toilet. Then my mother takes me back downstairs and sits me in front of my plate again. I stay in the darkened dining room, facing that horrible fish in its horrible mustard sauce that I refuse to eat.

The next day, after my father's morning routine, he says, 'Right, we'll take it away for lunchtime. You can eat it later.' At supper that evening the fish comes back, but only half the quantity. It's doable, I eat it. The hatchet has been buried until next Friday.

I'm prepared to start over. Or rather, Mathilde is prepared to start over. Maude is a pathetic failure; she trembles with fear and obeys. But Mathilde is a warrior; she's the one putting up a fight. I met her in *The Red and the Black*, and she dazzled me. I adore her energy, her passion, her uncompromising nature. She would sacrifice her life for her ideals. She has become my secret friend, encouraging me and backing me up. One time my father launched into a lecture about the name Maude spelled with or without the letter 'e'. Maud without an 'e' is derived from

Madeleine. Madeleines are crybabies. But Maude with an 'e' comes from Mathilde. I don't know whether it's true, but I immediately see myself somehow related to the courageous, intelligent and beautiful Mathilde. Now I'm not only Louis Didier's daughter, I'm Mathilde's twin sister. And she comes to the fore every time I have to wage a battle.

One thing Mathilde will not tolerate is when my father wants me to play the accordion for guests, whether it's just Albert and Rémi when they're having an aperitif, or one of our rare Freemason visitors. My father must know by now that I've never agreed to be his performing monkey. One morning he invites Raymond in for a Ricard. Not only do I have to wait on this pig, but now my father is telling me to play 'Sous les Ponts de Paris'. I refuse. He insists, I hold my ground; he gets angry and starts shouting. I don't recall what he says but Mathilde sees red. I grab my accordion and throw it at his face. I receive a good caning on my back and sixty hours of accordion practice on top of my normal schedule: 'You can go to bed an hour later and get up an hour earlier for a month,' he tells me.

It's a heavy punishment. But let it be known that Mathilde will not play the accordion for Raymond.

The Calf

The Killer's quarterly visits are becoming an obsession of mine as I find it increasingly hard to play the hypocritical role of soothing the poor condemned calf. In the lead-up to the Killer's visit, I picture myself freeing the doomed animal and making the most of those few minutes when the gates to the house are open for the delivery truck to run away with the calf. But when the day comes, the calf is always treacherously killed.

This time when the calf is chained up, I notice that the hook is smaller than usual. As soon as I'm left alone with the animal I try to release the hook. It works! I push the calf towards the open gate, urging it under my breath: 'Run, get out!' But it starts lurching in every direction, making an indescribable noise. The Killer runs after it, yelling. My mother screams at me to catch it. My father, who must have been woken by the noise, appears at his window and fires shots in the air. The calf runs into the electric fencing, leaping about frantically, and panics more and more.

In the end the Killer catches it. We now have to wait twenty-four hours for the animal to calm down again before it's killed. No one saw me release the snap hook so I'm not punished. But I'm consumed with shame for failing to save the poor creature and causing it even more terror instead.

I don't know whether this is something to do with Mathilde's rebellions, whether it's a roundabout way of bringing her to heel and silencing her, but my father has taken a pair of crutches from his cupboard and has started behaving as if he's handicapped. He hasn't fallen or injured himself and, even though he could walk unaided perfectly easily, I now have to support him if he wants to walk a few paces. I have to help him sit down, and help him on and off the toilet. While we tend to him in the morning and the evening, he now does absolutely nothing for himself. He doesn't lift his buttocks when my mother and I have to put on his pants. He doesn't raise his legs to make it easier for me to put on his socks. Every day I also have to massage his feet, which smell horrible and make me feel sick, with their long black nails. I feel guilty for being such a bad daughter, but at the same time I hate him. He can feel my hatred; he wants to 'tame' me.

It is summertime and we are having lunch out on the verandah. I am asked to cut a piece of old Dutch cheese that is so hard I struggle to get the knife through it. Irritated, my mother takes the knife from me and accidentally cuts herself. They both fly off the handle, saying I am responsible for her injury. My father tells me he is going to give me a punishment 'that will hurt'. All of a sudden I snap. I pick up the knife and drive it as hard as I can into

197

my other hand on the cheeseboard. I scream with all my might, 'Go on, then! What are you going to do to me now?' His eyes bore right through me. I don't look away. He can go ahead and kill me, I won't back down. I don't know how long this goes on; I still have the knife stuck in my hand. Finally, he gives in; he is the one who gives in. 'Go and get the whisky,' he says to my mother, 'and get yourself a bandage while you're at it.'

'Yes, that's right!' I bellow at my mother. 'Go and get the whisky. If there's something stronger, bring that too. If you like I'll pour some on your cut too.' She comes back with the bottle of Johnnie Walker. I draw the knife out of my hand and pour the whisky over the wound, which bleeds profusely. The whisky is dribbling onto the ground but I don't give a damn. I'm still staring at my father. He can't make me look away.

Eventually I go back to my piano and the keys end up smeared with blood. Mathilde is pleased, but there is something bothering me. As I poured the whisky I noticed something in the depths of my father's blazing eyes. I saw a hint of…pride. And now I'm suddenly not so satisfied with my rebellion. Am I not giving him exactly what he wants: a display of my strength, courage, determination and power? What if deep down I'm just a pathetic puppet who doesn't realize she's still just obeying his mental orders?

I don't know whether he's manipulating me. I don't know whether I have control of my own actions. My infuriation is indescribable. I dwell on this as I pick up fallen twigs on the lawn before mowing the grass. My father is nearby, sitting on his wooden crate. My back hurts from bending over, so I stand up. But this is forbidden: I must neither put a knee to the ground, which would be lazy, nor stand up. My father roars at me furiously. I pick up a long earthworm, which squirms between my fingers. I pretend to fling it at him and he ducks aside. Then, with a malicious glint in my eye, I dangle the worm above my face and drop it into my mouth. I chew it, looking him right in the eye. 'You can't do anything to me,' I yell. 'You'll never be able to do anything!'

My heart is beating wildly. I can't ride the wave of anger for much longer. I'm trying to swallow the worm but it turns my stomach. Every inch of me is shaking from the inside and I feel out of my depth, as if I'm losing my mind. Whatever I do, I end up harming myself. Will I never get out of this hell? I bend over to continue picking up twigs. I feel I'm in terrible danger. Help, I am going mad. My mother is right: all I'm good for is the asylum in Bailleul.

From my father's office I steal a small penknife I had noticed in a bottom drawer. I hide it under the carpet in my bedroom. That night I open it and look at it: it's old and the blade is worn. During the war my father knew people who would rather slit their own wrists than give in to the enemy. That's what I want to do now; then he will know that I see him as the enemy. I draw the knife backwards and forwards across my wrist. It breaks the skin but my veins slide beneath the blade, unharmed. Is it because it's too blunt? Or because I'm not pressing hard enough? I can feel a strong instinct battling against what I have decided to do. But I'm so desperate to get out of here...

Although nothing is changing in my life, I get the feeling something important is going on outside. We now hardly ever hear trains passing on the railroad tracks just fifty metres from the house. There are fewer trucks on the main road too. At night there is almost total silence. 'Jeannine,' my father says, 'call the co-op tomorrow and ask to have forty kilos of sugar and twenty litres of cooking oil delivered.' He says we must open the freezers as little as possible because we're likely to have power cuts. There's a generator that usually takes over if that happens, but we still need to keep the temperature of the freezers down as much as possible. He decides we should eat eggs for lunch and supper to avoid taking meat from the freezers.

What kills me is that Raymond now comes three times more often than usual. Apparently there are strikes in the port of Dunkirk, so he's not going to work. When we have our aperitif he talks to my father about 'events in Paris', students in the streets and people throwing cobblestones. It reminds me of Gavroche from *Les Misérables*. But my father avoids the subject. 'And your wife, how is she?' Or 'When do you think we should prune the trees?' The situation would be almost exciting if the diabolical Raymond weren't here just waiting for an opportunity to corner me. I can't bear it any longer, I want him to go back to work. How much longer is this strike going to last?

The Key

Winter is over but all the shutters overlooking the street are still closed. Never again will I see the workers walking to the Cathelain factory, nor the trucks setting off for England. My father issues the same instruction for all the ground-floor shutters that open onto the garden. The large downstairs rooms are now huge mausoleums filled with shadows.

As all of the life gradually drains out of the house, my father intensifies his inspections and searches. He never does the work himself but appears with no warning in my bedroom or my mother's and says, 'Now, take the covers off the bed.' He watches while we strip back the blankets, untuck the sheets and turn over the mattress...Then he nods at us to make the bed again and leaves. This can happen once a year or three times a month. I don't know what it is he's looking for. I think he mostly wants to create a mood of uncertainty. My mother is irritated that she is treated the same as I am. She doesn't say anything but it's obvious from her abrupt movements.

My parents haven't spoken to me for six weeks, as punishment for knocking over a pile of plates and, more to the point, almost giving my father a heart attack. I think I'm beginning to prefer these periods, when their disdain for me is so obvious, to the times when it is distilled into subtle soul-destroying slights.

I resume the habit of making vicious scratches on my thighs and arms. I also wind the cords of the thick curtains around my arms, wrists, thighs or calves. I pull them as tight as I can; sometimes I take a deep breath and pull tighter, until the pain knocks the breath out of me. I stop when I can't pull any harder. Now if I'm weeding the garden, I grasp stinging nettles and thistles with my bare hands. I no longer have any fear of pain because I'm the one inflicting it and can decide when it stops. My parents can see my hands are full of thorns but they make no comment.

I now know what I want to be when I grow up: not 'master of the world' but a 'surgeon of the head'. I've just finished reading Albert Camus's *The Plague* and, thanks to Dr Rieux, I understand that the mind can suffer just as much as the body. Since reading *The Idiot* I've had a burning desire to cure the wonderful Prince Myshkin's epilepsy. 'Doctors are asses,' my father always says. I wouldn't know because I've never met one. When I'm sick, my father looks after me with doses of white wine and a few Aspro. But the doctors I come across in books make my heart swell in admiration. Take Balzac's *The Country Doctor*—now there's a truly good man who won't settle for healing the body alone: he also helps the village live healthily, grow and become more attractive. That's what I would call a Being of Light.

The things I read are starting to rub off on me; I'm a melting pot of ideas, characters and stories. When my mother leaves me alone to do my homework, I turn to writing a sort of poem-novel whose hero is a bird that perches on the highest branch of the Australian poplar tree that sits on the grounds. From up there he watches the inhabitants who live in this weird house. Seeing the ducks swimming in the pond at the poplar's feet, he assumes they're masters of the house and that they have a zoo with lions (Linda), zebras (Périsaut) and giraffes (my parents and me). The bird wonders how these animals ended up so far from their natural habitats.

I'm rather pleased with my story, which I think is both entertaining and instructive. My mother, who makes me write essays, might enjoy it. I so wish she could see that I'm not as bad as she thinks. I decide to dedicate my poem-novel to her. When she reads it, maybe she'll stop hating me.

During my French lesson I hand it to her, a little apprehensive. Surprised, she glances over the piece of paper, scanning the text. Then throws it back in my face. 'When I see everything your imagination can come up with, how do you expect me ever to believe you're telling the truth?' In my mother's opinion, imagination and lies are one and the same. I can also tell she's horribly offended to have been compared to a giraffe. I'm very upset and try to explain that to a little bird she would surely look extremely tall. 'Seeing as you seem to have time to waste, I'll go and get the orange book for you and you can do some arithmetic exercises for us…' I back down. I won't be dedicating anything else to her.

But stories keep proliferating inside my head. They make me

almost giddy and I need to get them out. I steal some onion-skin paper from my father's desk and in the evenings I sit up in bed and cover the paper with tight rows of writing. Before going to sleep, I fold the paper in two and slide it between the rug and the carpet on the stairs. My parents tread on that step every morning, unaware of what I've hidden there, and it makes me shiver with a mixture of delight and fear.

But this system is too risky. To get to the staircase I have to pass my mother's bedroom door and she might hear me. I start looking for a hiding spot in my bedroom, and notice that the base of my wardrobe is about eighty centimetres from the floor. I lift up a plank to find that it is resting on a bed of bricks. I decide to dig a hiding place underneath.

First I have to attack the mortar around a brick. I steal the key to a second-floor bedroom, and it turns out to be strong enough to scratch away at the mortar. I work on this every evening. I put the loose chunks in my pocket and throw them away in the garden the next day. It doesn't take long to loosen the joints between the bricks. Now I need a tool hefty enough to tackle the bricks but small enough to fit in the gaps between them.

There's no way I can use one of my father's tools, which hang in front of their own silhouettes painted above the workbench. I think of the large key Raymond sometimes brings, which he has used to hurt me. Oh, that one! It would be perfect for digging out bricks. I want it. I'm going to get it from him. Every time he comes, I find an excuse to go into the greenhouse near the chicken coop, where he leaves his jacket. I rummage through his pockets, but there are no keys. I don't give up, though, and after many long weeks, luck smiles on me: the keys are there. I take them, then I dig a hole in the ground and bury them.

I've taken a huge risk, but what jubilation I feel! I know that losing them matters to Raymond. It's not just that he won't be able to get home this evening, but that he'll have to explain to his employers—the Dunkirk Council—what he's done with the key to the municipal stores…I hope they take a fat deduction from his wages. In the meantime, I watch Raymond's desperation with covert but intense pleasure: he's running all over the vast estate, frantically trying to find his keys.

As soon as I can, I dig up the key ring, remove the big key and throw the rest into the latrines in the garden. Raymond's key proves to be the perfect tool. Over several months, I dig at the bricks by night and empty my pockets by day. I'm Edmond Dantès and Abbot Faria rolled into one. Nothing can have a hold over me now that I'm working towards my spiritual escape. When the hiding place is big enough to hold my manuscripts and a flashlight, Raymond's key joins the others at the bottom of the latrines.

My mother must be aware on some level that I'm carrying out illicit activities. Now she's making her own searches, unbeknownst to my father. She's a far more tenacious inspector than he is: she overturns drawers, empties the closet, looks under the rug and behind the skirting boards. She is convinced I'm hiding something. But my cache is undetectable. When she's had enough of these fruitless searches, she turns to me and says, 'Don't you worry, I'll find it.'

The Flying Machine

Shakespeare is not an author. He is actually many different authors, five to be precise. Five Initiates (the same as in the 'just and perfect' Freemason Lodges), who littered those famous plays with coded messages that no layperson would ever detect. This was the surest way of perpetuating their ideas throughout the ages without risking censorship. Similarly, his Globe Theatre in London was a symbolic site loaded with energies. It was built on a polygonal base like a baptistery in order to radiate hidden ideas and further England's supremacy. My father makes me read lots of Shakespeare plays—*Henry IV, Richard III, King Lear, Coriolanus, Hamlet,* et cetera—in the original English. I don't understand any of it and I'm sure he doesn't either. But that doesn't matter; he says these blind readings still feed my mind very effectively. I'm more fascinated by the magnificent books printed on paper so thick that the letters seem to be engraved onto them. There is in this room a serene literary aura that I find soothing. Perhaps my father is right, perhaps the plays really are nourishing my mind.

He shows me other beautiful books, like those devoted to Leonardo da Vinci's inventions. I stroke their gilded bindings and my fingers can almost read their titles embossed in the leather. I stop short when I come to some bewitching drawings that my brain struggles to decipher. My father explains that Leonardo designed a flying machine long before planes were invented, and he even drew a blueprint for a helicopter. He was a genius and a very great Initiate, and he enlightened Francis I of France and managed to push back the tide of religious obscurantism. As the reincarnation of Beings of Light, he knew how best to use energies. His particular gift was his total mastery of the 'divine proportion' found in every animate and inanimate aspect of the universe, a proportion known as the 'golden ratio'. The parts of the human body conform to it, as do pentagons and pentagrams. The Egyptians followed this ratio when they built the pyramids, and Hiram of Tyre also used it in building Solomon's Temple.

My father says Leonardo da Vinci is among us still, through a series of reincarnations, and lives in Venice where he runs secret Lodges. I'm dazzled by the man's art, his intelligence and the breadth of his knowledge. How does he manage to remember everything when he's reincarnated? I feel ashamed that I can't remember anything and have no recollections of my former lives. I'd so love to meet da Vinci. I wonder if my father knows how to find him?

It must be wonderful to be so intelligent! Maybe my father's right. If I become a superhuman I might be of interest to people like Leonardo da Vinci. And I'd be released from the torment inside my head when I don't understand what's being asked of me. I need to pull myself together! First I must stop being such a softie. I decide that I won't look at Linda when I let her out. And when I shut her in I won't apologize to her or indulge her with petting. I put my program into operation. Linda looks up longingly for eye contact. I throw her a harsh 'Get out!' I can feel my heart breaking at the thought of what this is doing to her. But I hold out, gritting my teeth. Until the next morning, that is, when all my resolve melts with just one look at her. I tell her I'm sorry and hate myself for what I did. She doesn't bear any grudges, though—she's overjoyed to have me back.

But how do superhumans rise above their emotions? This question tortures me for weeks. The only suffering I can inflict is on myself. I punish myself for my sentimentality. I rip up some of my secret notes on onion-skin paper; I even contemplate tearing up the *Hungarian Rhapsody* score. In my mind, there's a battle between the half of me that says, 'No! That *Rhapsody* is Madame Descombes, you can't do that!' and the other half that retorts, 'Oh, really? Stop your pathetic excuses!'

Then one day, I have no idea why, the tussling abruptly stops. Was a meditation on death unusually tough? Did a test of courage come at the wrong time? Whatever it is, my fascination suddenly evaporates. I see my father as he truly is: a friendless, loveless man, who never gives or receives any kindness, and who even terrorizes animals. I look at my mother and see a woman who can't even speak freely to her own husband, can't use his first name, and has to listen to her radio in secret. Is that the path to enlightenment? It's the exact opposite of da Vinci's flying machine! My father is not trying to fly; he shoots at birds in the sky and chooses to stay cloistered in this ghastly place. But I want to be free, I want to fly away. If that means living outdoors, well, that's fine by me. If it means not having any food, so what? The only sustenance that matters is the love in my dog's eyes and the hope of meeting people who dare to truly live. I can't stop my father, my 'thought master', from filling me with his gibberish...but in my mind I'm no longer bound by his world of so-called superhumans.

Luckily I have music and books to calm the pandemonium inside my head. In the evenings I re-read *Les Misérables*, and it does me good. I feel an almost physical pleasure in my brain, as if something were opening up inside it, transporting me to a different world filled with different stories. I know these stories are made up, but I believe they're very close to real life. When the electricity is cut off, I rest the book on my chest and rapturously remember the final passages. When I re-read *The Hunchback of Notre-Dame*, I'm completely overcome. I'm in love for the first time, and my love is Quasimodo. I am moved by his hidden beauty. Lying wide-eyed in the dark, I picture myself walking proudly on his arm. As we pass by, people turn to look, suddenly dazzled as they see his beauty for the first time.

Friendship

After mowing the lawn my mother and I rake the grass cuttings into little heaps. My father is in charge of 'operation bonfire', which is tricky in a part of the world where the grass is rarely dry. He digs several holes into the pile of cuttings and pours petrol into them. Then he rolls pages of newspaper into the shape of little torches, lights these and throws them into the holes.

One day, one of the paper torches misses its target. A tongue of flame leaps up my father's legs; he starts hopping around like a goat, contorting frantically as he tries to put out the flames on the bottom of his pants. My mother and I are paralyzed, astonished by this dancing jumping jack. For years now my father has hardly even walked, as if he had some serious handicap with his legs. Since he's been using crutches so much, we were worried he would ask for a wheelchair next.

Finally, through gritted teeth, my mother mutters, 'Your father is just a pathetic fraud. I hate that man.' She is waiting for me to agree with her but I'm too frightened she'll use my words against me. 'Of course, you're always on his side,' she snaps.

'What the hell are you doing?' my father bellows. 'Light the fire now!' I snap out of my dazed state and do as I'm told, filled with boundless sadness that when my mother reached out to me I missed my chance to reach back.

In front of my father I shrivel up in fear, but when my mother talks negatively about him, she really messes with my mind. It's usually when we're walking downstairs to join him out in the grounds or when he's 'summoned' both of us together. 'I hate that man,' she mutters. 'What is all this crap about? Your father never got further than high school. Who does he think he is?' But as soon as we're with him, she becomes small and obedient, all 'yes, of course' and 'I'll do it right away'. It's bewildering, as if she's forcing me to do the splits emotionally, like when she pushes down on my shoulders in the gymnasium to splay my legs apart.

I sometimes wonder whether these rants of hers are just a trap to corner me into confiding my negative thoughts. But no, her hatred is genuine. Particularly when it includes me. These moments strike me like lightning. 'Who do you think you are?' she spits suddenly, and I stiffen with fear and confusion. It's as if someone is whispering things in her ear that make her angry. 'Oh, you think you're your father's daughter, do you?' she says bitterly. 'Well, you'll get what you want…I'm only stuck here because of you. It's all your fault.' I'm so shaken that it's hard to hold back my tears. That's when she hits me with: 'Stop the charade!'

At other times she sings my father's praises, listing the

sacrifices he's made all these years. It's for my sake that he paid for her long study programs, so that I can reap the benefits now. I'm an ungrateful daughter, failing to live up to his expectations.

I just don't understand what she wants and I don't know how to satisfy her. I wish she would say, 'He's keeping us both prisoner and we should work together to escape.' I think I would even prefer her to say frankly that she loves him, that she does everything for him and that if it doesn't suit me, then tough. That would be clear, at least I would know what I'm up against and would stop having my heart cut to ribbons by her sudden changes of attitude and inconsistencies.

After all, I don't expect much from her anymore. Every day I continue to prepare my new hiding place in my room. I silently retrieve all my onion papers that I slipped under the stair rugs, and I re-read my stories before hiding them again. The one I find most moving is set in the trenches during the 1870 Franco-Prussian war. A Prussian soldier called Leopold is injured. Jean-Baptiste, a Frenchman, launches himself on Leopold to kill him. But just as he is about to bayonet him, they make eye contact and Jean-Baptiste can't bring himself to kill the injured man. He deserts his command, carries him away from the front lines, and tends to his wounds. The two men don't speak each other's languages but they communicate with their eyes and gestures. They are eventually caught by the French army and condemned to death. They face the firing squad with their hands locked together in a handshake. Infuriated, the officer gives the order to fire. The two friends are still holding hands as they fall. Everyone is touched by the story of their friendship, even the Prussians. Cheers for Jean-Baptiste ring out from the Prussian trenches while French soldiers chant Leopold's name. Soldiers on both sides throw down their weapons and venture towards each other to shake hands, emulating Jean-Baptiste and Leopold's final gesture. There are mutinies on both sides and the war comes to an end. A 'Leopold—Jean-Baptiste' treaty is signed between France and Prussia, which becomes a pact for world peace. The First and Second World Wars never happen.

As I fall asleep I come up with a title for my story: 'Friendship'.

Thales' Theorem

My father has always told me I would start my period at thirteen. I'm thirteen now and today I found blood in my underwear. I wait till lesson time before telling my mother. She drops everything and goes to tell my father, then reappears with a packet of maxi pads and hands them to me without a word of explanation. Luckily the instructions are printed on the packaging. She finishes the lesson early and says, 'Go to the ballroom and wait for your father.'

I am nervous. God knows what I will hear. When I walk into the ballroom I'm struck by the abundance of light streaming in: before going upstairs, my mother opened all the shutters that have been closed for at least a year. I stand and wait. My father makes his entrance, clearly moved almost to tears. He goes over to the bar, fills one of his precious crystal glasses with Chivas whisky and brings it to me. I'm rooted to the spot with surprise: my father has never gone to the trouble of getting a glass, holding a bottle or pouring a drink for anyone, ever.

'Sit down,' he says. 'You're a woman now. That calls for celebration. Drink it all.'

While I drink down the whisky one burning mouthful at a time, he goes back over the teachings he has already given me about menstruation. Firstly, stomach cramps associated with periods exist only in the minds of hysterical women. Secondly, periods last only two and a half days, three at the most, and recur exactly every twenty-eight days. And thirdly, they constitute a period of receptivity: 'You are particularly sensitive to good energies, as well as bad. So no one must ever know when you are menstruating. You should also stay away from animals because they can sense it and they could unwittingly reveal the information to your enemies.'

Because of this greater openness and sensitivity, I must be even more selective about what goes into my brain: I mustn't read anything 'light' or listen to advertising. I should feed my mind only intelligent material and meditations with the spirits. But there's nothing for me to worry about. I'll be regular as clockwork just like my mother. He will keep a record of my dates and ensure I won't get 'polluted'.

My father also explains the special power a woman has during her period. Her blood, which is shed naturally, is the power of life itself, of renewal. Men don't have this power because their blood is shed only through violence. They therefore don't have women's capacity for personal renewal, so their energies dwindle inexorably—except, of course, in the case of great Initiates, but that's another story. Most religions are afraid of this female power. Judaism, for example, would have women believe they are impure, in order to distance them from their powers. Similarly, the reign of matter makes them believe they have stomach cramps. I, however, must avoid making these mistakes and maximize my powers by fully absorbing my father's teachings.

Maybe it's because I'm a woman now or maybe my father is tired of hearing my scales all day long, but this summer he has commissioned the construction of a 'music pavilion', carefully insulated against cold and sound. All my instruments will be kept here and this is where I will practise. Since having my period, I've also done less work as an apprentice bricklayer. My mother is often nearby and I have the feeling she is keeping an eye on my contact with Albert and Rémi.

My mother still quakes at the thought of my homework coming back from the correspondence school with bad marks, or even average ones. My father is very quick to reprimand her harshly in front of me. She has managed to find a loophole that allows her to obtain the answer sheets early: she now sends the examiners my 'homework', which consists of the answer sheets that she has made me copy out, making a few minor changes. My marks are now consistently excellent. My father is satisfied and my mother relieved. I should be too, but deep down I resent her. I couldn't care less about good marks. I want to learn. 'I'm warning you,' she says, 'if you talk to your father about this, I'll tell him you're the one who's making the corrections. And that's the truth, anyway!'

Eighteen or nineteen out of twenty isn't good enough. She wants to impress my father and flaunt her extraordinary teaching skills. I have to shine. She made me complete the seventh and eighth grades in one year. At thirteen and a half, I'm already in ninth grade. That's easy when you're just copying out the answer sheets, but we both know it's fake. I am increasingly angry; she is depriving me of the true education that is absolutely necessary in order for me to grow and become strong enough to one day take off. My 'pure' and 'superior' education is phony. The protection I'm meant to benefit from in this house is phony. My father's grandiose teachings are phony. My whole life is a charade. When I ask her for proper lessons she says, 'You'll just have to learn from the answer sheets. All it takes is intelligence and will.'

When it comes to maths, it's a disaster. She doesn't understand any of it and is no help at all. I toil over the manuals but without outside help I can't get anywhere. Because my work is always excellent, I can't even turn to the teachers at the correspondence school. I can't find help anywhere. One day we come to the lesson about Thales' theorem. I read the lesson and don't understand a word of it. I desperately draw various triangles, but nothing makes sense. My father knows his pyramids, so I could ask him, but my mother strictly forbids it. I'm devastated. If I can't do maths, that means no medical studies. Goodbye to my dream of becoming a 'surgeon of the head', goodbye to my medical and healer heroes...I'm condemned to being shut away here forever. Even if I manage to get out, by some miracle, I won't know how to do anything.

Goodbye, Linda

Linda is nearly eleven, very old for a German Shepherd. She is lame and her eyesight is failing. In spite of everything, my father still wants her to be locked in her kennel. When I let her out in the evenings I sometimes notice she's had a little 'accident'. She looks up at me with such shame in her eyes that my heart constricts. No, it's not your fault, Linda, you shouldn't be behind this fence.

One evening I find bloodstained diarrhoea in her kennel. I tell my mother right away and she is worried, but we mustn't tell my father because he's sick. We don't know how to make Linda more comfortable. She has stopped eating and is visibly getting worse. My father decides to take to his bed, so now we're confined to his room for goodness knows how many days.

Périsaut won't leave Linda's side for a minute. When I go down to feed them he's always right there with his head inside the kennel.

We spend a second night attending to my father. The silence is suddenly broken by wailing. It is Périsaut whinnying helplessly at the top of his lungs. I can see my mother is listening too. I want to say something but she whispers, 'Be quiet, you'll wake your father.' My heart is pounding. I know; I understand. Linda is dead, and Périsaut is mourning her. I remember how desolate Linda was when Arthur died. I'm overwhelmed by the same pain, a grieving child's pain, all over again.

When he wakes, my father sends me to see what's going on in the garden. I walk down the steps from the terrace. Périsaut is there pawing the ground; he comes up to me, turns back towards the kennel, then comes back towards the kitchen again. I can see his distress but I just can't seem to walk any further. Until I've seen her, Linda is still alive. Eventually I make it to the kennel. The floor is covered in blood and she's lying stretched out with blood all over her hindquarters.

When I go in to share the news, my mother looks upset. We set off to dig a grave over by the aviaries, not far from where Arthur is buried. It has rained a lot recently, so the earth is soft. Périsaut follows and watches us work. My mother locks him in the stables, worried he'll want to dig up Linda the way Linda tried to dig up Arthur. We can hear his sorrowful little whinnies as we bury his friend. When I open the door to let him out, he stays in the stable, as if doing penance. My mother and I have to spend a third night watching over my father. Périsaut cries right through until morning.

I'm too heartbroken to shed tears. It pains me to think of the life Linda had. I don't see why, with such a big house and such large grounds, the poor dog had to be tormented.

My father decides we need another dog. He arranges to have another German Shepherd delivered, a female, of course, and she'll be called...Linda. Are all beings interchangeable as far as the great Initiates are concerned?

The following Saturday my father sends me down to the cellar to fetch a tool. Raymond is right on my heels. Just as he slips behind me to grab me, I turn around and face him. I don't say a word but look him right in the eye. While I stare at him, I have flashbacks of the past: his arm outstretched, saying 'Come closer,' smiling at me. It was a strange smile but, being unused to smiles, I couldn't recognize the toxic ones. 'Come here, next to me,' he said, with his hands on my shoulders. 'A cuddle?' he offered. I ought to have been happy, since I longed for someone to take me in their arms. But I wasn't. I didn't like the smell of him or his weird breathing. He would rub up against me hard, and I hated it. The next few times he would go further, much further. The full force of my hatred rises up inside me. Now all the horror, the shame and fear of these last seven years, all the threats made and reiterated, they're all swept aside by violent rage. I stare at him and he starts to look frightened. What can he be afraid of? That I'll tell someone? Who could I tell? No one would help me. But he doesn't know that. All he can see is my fury. He backs away. He'll never come near me again. Never. He'll be the one having nightmares tonight.

As I lie in bed that evening the dam holding back the tears since Linda's death finally gives way. I cry for her, and I cry because I had to lose her in order finally to be free of that vampire.

Guardian of the Temple

As they do every summer, the builders return to construct new buildings on the grounds: a bread oven and a very small circular room that my father calls the 'bar', where he now spends most of his waking hours. He has an intercom set up in there so he can hear what's going on in the music pavilion. Safe in the knowledge that he can monitor what I'm doing, he spends most days copying out German detective novels, writing them onto sheets of card-stock with a fountain pen in an increasingly wobbly hand.

From one day to the next, my father's crutches disappear. Every morning at 9 a.m. he heads over to 'the bar' where he spends his day. Every evening at 8 p.m. he heads back. A lavatory and a small kitchen have been added along with the bread oven. From now on it is there that my mother cooks and where we eat our meals.

I don't understand why my father stays confined in that small space full of smoke from the cigarillos he chainsmokes. He's only seventy now, but behaves like a very old man. I have to sit him down on the toilet seat and help him pull up his pants afterwards. I'm ashamed of his smell, ashamed of being ashamed of him, ashamed of hating him, and of being ungrateful for his 'sacrifices'. I'm getting migraines from the boiling cauldron of contradictory emotions in my head.

I think my father, the king of knocking his drinks down in one go, now has trouble holding his liquor. He stumbles and has to be supported on his way back to the house. He puts this down to his 'failing health', but could it be due to a serious increase in consumption? I notice he pours himself big glasses of Chivas all through the day and frequently uncorks excellent champagnes. Twice a year he has hundreds of bottles of fine wine and spirits delivered. It's as if he's in a hurry to drink his money away.

He washes less and less, sometimes every two weeks, sometimes every three. When he takes a bath I'm supposed to use the bathwater after him. What I actually do is make splashing noises by flicking my face washer around in the tub. Since my father finally had basins installed in the bedrooms, I use mine to wash every night. I run only a thin stream of water to be sure the pipes don't make any noise.

Normally I have to go to the bar at eleven-thirty every day for my 'German lesson'. But today, for some reason, I've been summoned to the ballroom. This time the shutters are all closed. There's a solemn atmosphere. My father is in pride of place in the centre of the room, looking serious, portentous. He gestures for me to sit on a footstool in front of him. My mother has also been summoned and is leaning against the door behind me.

'You know that you are the guardian of the temple,' he says. An alarm bell sounds inside my head. 'When I die, I shall be buried in the garden. And it is you who will watch over my tomb forever.'

The more he talks the more the panic rises inside me.

'You won't be alone. I shall visit you, I shall always be by your side to continue my teaching.' He tells me where his tomb should be: where the bench in the garden currently stands, facing the verandah.

On my way out I notice that my mother is ashen; she looks as shaken as I feel. We shut ourselves away in the schoolroom and whisper despairingly, 'It can't be! It's not possible! Not forever!'

Like me, she had always known that my mission would be to 'guard' my father's memory after his death, but we thought it wouldn't be for a long time. She didn't realize I would have to guard his tomb and that his physical remains would stay on the property.

'But I'm going to run away,' I say. That has always been my mother's obsessive fear: that I will run away and leave her here to face my father's rage.

'No, you won't! That's not going to happen, I won't agree to that.' It's almost as if she's begging me not to abandon her.

That evening I mull over this latest announcement. Does he really think I'll want to watch over his tomb and see him emerge from it after his death? Does everyone who is reincarnated need their daughter to watch over their tomb? Leonardo da Vinci didn't have a daughter. Besides, before contemplating starting a new life, you need to make something of this one. I've never seen either of my parents do anything worthwhile. Great minds defend values—like justice in the case of Victor Hugo, and equality for Emile Zola. What does my father ever do, except copy out German detective stories that he doesn't even understand?

I struggle not to let him drag me down into this abyss with him. He doesn't really have a life; it's more like a living death, and we're drowning in his smells and filth. It's been twelve years now since he buried himself alive—taking us with him—behind the gates of this property. He can go ahead and build his mausoleum in the garden. He can put a pyramid on it if he likes. He can even take his wife into the hereafter with him, like the glorious pharaohs he's always talking about…

But I won't be guarding that tomb. I make myself a silent promise to myself that I won't.

What were you thinking...

Something exceptional is about to happen. In June I'm taking the French language section of my *baccalauréat*. Since my mother made me skip a year, things are progressing just as my father hoped: the French test at fifteen, the rest of the final-year *bac* at sixteen. My mother orders me a pantsuit in midnight blue velvet and new shoes. I also need an ID card so we have to go to the town hall in the village. My mother wears a scarf and dark glasses, and takes out a large handbag I haven't seen for years—not since we used to go and see Madame Descombes. We leave through the small garden gate: 'That way, we'll be more unobtrusive.' How long is it now since we've been outside? I try to count. Eight years, maybe nine? It's strange, the air almost smells different. I'm startled by a passing truck, which feels as if it's sucking me into its wake. We turn right and walk past houses with pretty pots of flowers hanging in front of open windows. I don't think I've ever seen flowers in pots. I'm so used to cemented pathways that I find it hard not to trip on the uneven paving stones and I have to slow down. But my mother is hurrying; I can tell she's anxious. Behind the houses there are fields as far as the eye can see. The horizon is so beautiful! No one should ever be deprived of a horizon.

On the main square in front of the church is the town hall with its red, white and blue flag, just like in books. A kind woman greets us and fills out a form: 'Eye colour?' she asks, looking at me, then says, 'Oh, don't you have pretty blue eyes.' On the way home we don't recognize the streets anymore, we go around in circles, incapable of finding our way. For a moment, I have a crazy idea that we could leave, the two of us, and never go back to the house. But my mother is in a complete panic. Her scarf has slipped off and she has bitten her lip so hard it's bleeding. Suddenly we hear a train. She almost runs to the railroad tracks; we need only follow them and we'll soon be at the main entrance to the house.

Before stepping through the gate, I take one last look up the road that runs parallel to the metal fence and leads to Saint-Omer, far, far away beyond the horizon.

My notification for the exam arrives: I have to be at Paul Hazard high school in Armentières at eight o'clock in the morning. My parents tell me what I have to do: go to the station, which is just 30 metres to the left outside our main gate, find the platform for trains heading to Lille, and get off at Armentières. From there I'll take a taxi to the high school.

The night before the exam I don't sleep at all. In the morning

I go out into the street alone because my mother has to stay by my father's side. Alone! But I'm so anxious I don't really feel like I'm outside. I look at my watch every ten seconds to check I'm doing as I've been told. Am I on the right platform? I feel so tiny I could disappear into the asphalt. But I also feel so big. I hate my size. I'm a giant compared to everyone else, and people are staring at me. I wonder fretfully whether I'll be able to open the door to the train, and decide to tag along behind some other passengers. I copy what they do, climb into the carriage after them and sit down behind them. During the journey another panicking thought gnaws at me: How long will the train stop at Armentières? How will I get out? And how will I find the high school? At Hazebrouck I watch closely as other passengers disembark. It doesn't look too hard.

As the train draws into Armentières a lot of passengers stand up all around me. Aha, I hadn't thought of that: I'm not the only one taking these exams. What a relief! I mingle happily with a group of teenagers and follow them without worrying, delighted that I don't need to look for this 'taxi' thing. I'm finally realizing the dream I've had my whole life: blending with the crowd, going with the flow, being like everyone else. I'm walking along with a group of high school kids! Still, I'm struggling to settle into their rhythm. They all seem to be walking in time, and I can't get my legs to adopt the same pace. In the end I count the beats, as I would with a piece of music; this helps and stops me from tripping. But why do I feel sad? Why do I feel so alone? I'm a breed apart, out of sync, weird in my too-big velvet jacket, my too-short pants and my shoes which, of course, are hurting me terribly. The other kids are in jeans, wear their hair loose, they're all chatting and laughing. They're beautiful and I'm ugly. We arrive at the high school and I walk through the gate; I should be brimming with happiness but I feel appallingly awkward and uncomfortable.

I find my desk, and when I turn over the exam paper I'm surprised to discover I have to choose between three different types of question. There's an essay (as I was expecting) and two other tests I don't recognize: a 'textual analysis' and a 'text summary'. The only one I know how to do is the essay, but I decide they must all be pretty much the same thing. I choose the 'textual analysis' because it's about a pretty poem, *'Si tu t'imagines, fillette'* ('What were you thinking, little girl').

I'm even more nervous about the oral exam. I'm not used to talking at all, particularly with strangers. My voice doesn't obey me; it wavers, croaks and squeaks. Sometimes no sound at all comes out. Luckily I'm examined on a Baudelaire poem that I love: *'Le parfum'* ('Perfume'). My examiner seems to like it too. I start off stammering but, thanks to the encouragement in her expression, my voice settles and in the end it almost feels as if we're having a conversation. When I arrive home my mother reads through the notes I made and seems satisfied.

The envelope containing my results arrives at last. Confident in her teaching skills, my mother opens it proudly. Disaster: I have a good 16/20 in the oral but in the written exam…2/20! My parents look at me as if I've murdered someone. I've just proved that I'm a 'walking disappointment'. All the same, my father asks to see the comments on my written exam: 'This is a fine philosophical essay, not a textual analysis.'

I pray my parents will understand that the education they're giving me is inadequate. I beg my mother to send me to boarding school. 'How dare you ask such a thing?' she says, sounding offended. 'Don't you know it would kill your father?'

Monsieur Molin

My father wants to buy a medium grand piano for the music pavilion. There's no question of his going to choose one in a store, so my mother makes some enquiries over the telephone. She eventually comes across a Monsieur André Molin, who runs the best music shop in Dunkirk, and he offers to come to the house to discuss our requirements. I think I'll always remember the sight of him. I open the door and there is a small man leaning on crutches. He is about sixty, has a bit of a paunch and kind eyes. He smiles at me and it feels as if a sunbeam is reaching right inside me. Even my father is captivated by his gentleness. He starts by inspecting our existing baby grand piano and is surprised to discover that my father never realized pianos need tuning. He defuses the problem with great tact: 'Oh, it only needs doing every once in a while. Particularly in a beautiful house like this.' As if the house could tune the piano!

My father is charmed and asks him to see to the job anyway, adding, 'If you could cast an eye over the other instruments as well...Besides the piano, Maude has been playing several other instruments for many years now: the accordion, the clarinet, the saxophone, the trumpet, the organ and the drums...' As this list gets longer, my head droops lower. I feel as if I'm shrinking, reduced to my role as a performing monkey. 'I sometimes make her study up to ten hours a day,' my father says, and the man gives a noncommittal 'hmm, hmm'. I can't bear to look at him.

'Bring the glasses, Maude,' my father says.

When I look up I notice that our visitor is peering at me with a sort of amazement mingled with concern. It's an expression I've seen before: when Madame Descombes saw scratches on my hands.

'You'll have a whisky, won't you,' my father says. It's nine o'clock in the morning; Monsieur Molin raises his eyebrows but hesitates for only a fraction of a second. While he stoically works his way through his glass, he tells us about his travels as a musician onboard the ocean liner *France*, where he ended up playing many different instruments. My father's eyes light up: since Yves vanished—after borrowing money from my father—it's been impossible to find a multi-instrument teacher.

'And do you play the accordion?' he asks.

'Of course!'

Just like that, Monsieur Molin is my new music teacher. And what a teacher! An extraordinary musician but also the personification of kindness. With him, even the accordion becomes a pleasure. I'm six inches taller than he is, but he calls me 'little one'—no one has ever called me that. He tells me about the musicians whose compositions I'm studying, and at what stage in their lives they wrote a particular piece. Music comes to life inside me; it's no longer just a succession of notes. Even *Crystal Pearls*, an accordion piece my father has insisted I learn, now feels poetic.

My teacher arrives, limping along on his crutches, for two four-hour sessions a week. We work in the music pavilion, mostly on piano and accordion. His ears are as sharp as mine and he too can hear the click on the intercom when my father decides to listen in on us. Then he speaks more sternly but softens his facial expression so much that we both smile as he scolds, 'No, really! You're just not making good enough progress on the accordion… If you came to my studio in Dunkirk you'd understand what a bit of hard work means. Then you'd get somewhere.'

I think Monsieur Molin understands. He has intuited that I am on the verge of imploding. I don't know how he worked it out as I haven't told him anything. He must have a sixth sense. He can tell just by looking at me, and I think he can read my father like a book. I think he has decided to help me and has hatched a plan to woo my father. At the end of the lessons, my mother comes to give him his envelope, and nudges him towards the side gate.

'Oh, but I must go say hello to Monsieur Didier,' he says and heads off towards the bar, chatting merrily as if he hasn't noticed my mother's disgruntled expression. Even though he's been officially warned by his doctor not to drink, he always agrees to have a glass of something. He must realize that my father's respect depends on it.

When the intercom clicks during our lessons, he has taken to saying harshly, 'I can see you have an easy life here. You'd have it tough if you came to practise under my orders at the studio. I'd get you playing the double bass. Oh, you'd suffer for it. And I'd make you clean all the instruments, and the floor too...' I have to stifle my laughter, he's going too far, it'll never work!

But it does. The next time he comes, my father asks him, 'Do you think the double bass would be a good idea for Maude?'

'For Maude? I hadn't thought of that, it's a very good idea.'

'In that case,' says my father, 'could you bring one next time?'

Monsieur Molin must be pleased with himself. Then my father asks him whether, to his knowledge, there were any double bass players in the concentration camps. He stands speechless for a moment, then says, 'Um, I'll find out...'

Monsieur Molin is my breath of fresh air. On my excursion to take the *bac*, I realized how out of step I am with the real world. I'm terrified this discrepancy is irreversible, that I'll only ever have a semblance of a normal life and will always be on the fringes. So I feel the blood draining from my face when Monsieur Molin says he has to take some time off for an operation.

'But I've brought you two Rachmaninoff preludes,' he says. 'You can start by sight-reading the one in C sharp minor, and we'll work on it together when I'm back on my feet.'

I throw myself wholeheartedly into Rachmaninoff. Even in my room at night, I stop my secret writing to play an imaginary keyboard. I spend hours at the piano with the accordion on my lap; as soon as I hear the intercom click my hands leap to the accordion. When it clicks off again I go back to the piano. By midsummer I've more or less worked out the prelude in C sharp minor and turn my attention to the one in G minor. It's harder and I end up thinking about it all the time. When my parents talk to me they sound far away.

Monsieur Molin comes back at last and I want to amaze him by playing both preludes. He certainly is amazed, but I can tell that he is also concerned. I beg him to order Rachmaninoff's Second Piano Concerto. 'Maybe do something else for a while,' he suggests. When I insist, he agrees, but on the condition that I also work on two other composers.

When he has to be away for a second operation to his hip following an infection, I throw myself into the concerto heart and soul. It is much longer than the preludes and I'm not up to it. I persist doggedly, becoming obsessed, losing myself in the notes, hearing them inside my head day and night. Luckily, Monsieur Molin comes back quite quickly and is alarmed to see the state I'm in: I'm playing too quickly, talking too quickly, struggling to control myself. And, to his astonishment, I put the accordion on my lap before playing the piano. It's become such a habit that I don't even know I'm doing it.

Very gently he starts telling me about Rachmaninoff, who suffered a four-year depression after the failure of his first concerto. He talks about Rimski-Korsakov, who was his master and role model. I could work on his *Flight of the Bumblebee*. I'd enjoy it, says Monsieur Molin. Enjoy—what a strange idea, I think. 'Oh, but watch out,' he adds. 'It's a difficult piece. And we could kill two birds with one stone because it's been adapted for the accordion. That'll please your father.'

I'm instantly charmed by *The Flight of the Bumblebee*, and I also discover Manuel de Falla: Monsieur Molin plays me his *Ritual Fire Dance* and I'm dazzled by it. He gradually draws me away from my obsession with Rachmaninoff. A few months later I return to the preludes and realize I'm playing them differently, more seriously. As for the Second Concerto, I give up on it with no regrets because we've now moved on to Liszt's *Hungarian Rhapsody*: my ultimate dream since losing Madame Descombes ten years ago.

Marie-Noëlle

A year later I take the train to Armentières again—filled with even more apprehension than last time—for my full *baccalauréat* exams. My mother has told me, 'If anyone asks why you're home-schooled, say you have very bad asthma and can't go to high school.' But no one asks.

German as first foreign language: I've studied Schiller and Goethe, but I'm confronted with modern texts that make my head spin. It's the same problem with English: I've worked on Shakespeare, but I'm supposed to tackle a subject taken from a book whose cover bears the American flag. The only consolation is the optional music paper: I play Rachmaninoff's Prelude in C Sharp Minor and the examiner exclaims, 'But you play beautifully! Why aren't you taking a music *baccalauréat?*' I didn't know there was such a thing.

In the History-Geography oral I happen to get one subject I know well, 'The Russian Campaign', and one I know less well, 'The development of Latin America'. The examiner sucks on his pipe as he listens to me talk, then seems to come to life and asks me about Brazil and King Pelé. I've never heard of a King Pelé.

'You do know Brazil are world champions thanks to Pelé?' he asks, raising an eyebrow. 'You don't? Or that the soccer World Cup just started in Germany?'

I'm speechless.

'Studying is all very well, young lady, but you also need to take an interest in the world around you. And anyway, it doesn't matter if you fail your *bac* at sixteen. In fact, it's better. It'll give you time to mature and develop a bit of curiosity.'

Unsurprisingly, my marks are terrible. Despite my 20/20 in music and 16/20 in philosophy, I've failed. My passport out of this place just expired. My dreams of studying at university instantly evaporate, and it feels as if the house is closing in around me. My parents give me the silent treatment; I can tell they're more disappointed by the failure of their teaching techniques than they are concerned about my future. But as much as I beg my mother to send me to boarding school, she always refers to the fatal effect this would have on my father. But what about me? Who would protect me from a far worse incarceration—in a lunatic asylum?

I drift from despondency to a sort of inner hysteria where my nerves start jumping beneath my skin. I have to do something. Writing stories and playing music aren't enough, I need movement. Since I've been outside it's as if I've developed a taste for some drug: I'm just dying to do it again.

When I go for walks in the grounds at night I feel increasingly drawn to the metal railings that fence us off from the road. High and forbidding, their spikes point skywards. When I look at them I keep seeing the images of impaled bodies that my father enjoys describing in lurid detail. All the same, I climb onto the low wall, grasp hold of the railings, heave myself up and clamber over those deadly spikes. I jump down onto the footpath: there, I'm on the other side. My God, it feels good, it really does smell different out here…I look at the road as it rises up towards the horizon. No, I don't want to die; this is what I want, to live. But I can't shake off my fear. I'm like a prisoner chained to a post, and I can only move as far as my chain will allow. Eventually, I climb back over the fence and return to my room, torn between my longing to breathe freely in the outside world and my towering fear.

As I come downstairs one morning, I notice an envelope in the letterbox, and I almost fall over backwards when I see my name written on it in pretty handwriting. No one has ever written to me. My hands shake with excitement. I see on the back of the envelope that it's from Marie-Noëlle, a girl I met during the *bac* exams, a girl full of joy and energy, and so pretty, her gorgeous black hair tied up in a ponytail. 'Hey, we could write each other,' she had said. 'Could I have your address?'

I open the envelope feverishly and unfold two whole pages covered on both sides with blue writing and little flowers drawn in the margins. Marie-Noëlle tells me she failed her *bac* but it doesn't matter, she's having a good summer anyway. So it is possible to fail your *bac* and not feel like a walking disappointment. I remember her saying she was married at seventeen, but she now tells me she no longer gets along with her husband—she's met another boy and they've kissed. Then she tells me about her holidays, about her 'Mum' and 'Dad', and how she's really glad to see them because she has so much to tell them. She hopes I'll write to her and that we'll see each other again. If I'd like to go and see her, her parents would be happy for me to come and stay at their holiday home.

I'm flabbergasted that she remembers me. Her happiness and exuberance are contagious. Her letter fills me with hope. It proves that life goes on after failing the *bac*, that love keeps going, that there are parents who keep talking to their daughters.

What could I write to her about? I don't have anything to tell her. Then I think, yes I do, I can tell her about the books I'm reading, about the garden and about Pitou, who's just died after a good long life. I can tell her how in recent weeks he turned into a 'lame duck', and how I loved his limping gait. I realize that, even cut off from the world, I have plenty to say, that life goes on everywhere. In my head I write her a letter several pages long: I don't have a lover but I'm in love with life, with nature, with newly hatched pigeon chicks…I ask my mother for some pretty paper and some stamps. First she demands to read Marie-Noëlle's letter and almost chokes: 'You've been out once and you've already got involved with the local prostitution ring! A girl who marries at seventeen is a prostitute! And she's kissed another boy too!'

'But she's getting a divorce…'

My mother confiscates the letter and strictly forbids me from contacting 'that filthy whore'.

I feel discouraged. What to do now? I am pacing in my cage and hitting the bars on all sides. I am both irritated and hurt by the grand speeches that my mother gives me during mealtimes.

'We wanted to mould you into someone perfect,' she says, 'and this is what we get. You're a walking disappointment.'

My father chooses this moment to subject me to one of his bizarre exercises: He slits a chicken's throat and demands that I drink its blood. 'It's good for the brain.'

No. Too much. Doesn't he realize I have nothing to lose now? That he's dealing with a kamikaze? No, he doesn't. He insists, reprimands, threatens…When he starts yelling in the deep voice that used to freeze my blood as a little girl, I explode: 'I said no! I won't drink your chicken blood, not today and not any day. And by the way, I won't watch over your tomb either. No way! And if I have to, I'll pour cement over it so no one can come back out of it. I know all about making cement, thanks to you!'

I am staring right into his eyes, holding his gaze. I know all about maintaining eye contact too—more than he does, it seems, because he is the one who looks away. I am about to collapse, but I've done it.

'You won't get out of it like that,' he says icily. 'I'm stronger than you.'

But he has lost.

A few days later he says, 'Don't go thinking you're off the hook. Even if you refuse to watch over me, I'll never leave you and you'll never leave me. Whether you like it or not, I control your mind.'

Monsieur Delataille

I have started double bass lessons with Monsieur Molin. I adore the instrument's woody smell, the sensuality of the bow vibrating over the strings. What a pleasure it is learning to play an instrument without violence or threats. Twice a week he continues to 'sing the praises' of the implacably severe music studio in Dunkirk where he teaches. When he goes for a drink after the lesson, my father has taken to asking him whether it would speed up my progress if I learned 'somewhere else'. Monsieur Molin isn't very forthcoming: 'Maybe...it might be possible...But maybe not.' This is exactly what it takes to make my father insist he accept me in his classes immediately. And he definitely shouldn't go easy on me. Monsieur Molin pretends to accept against his wishes: 'Well, okay, I'll see your daughter at 2 p.m. tomorrow at my store at 11 rue Nationale.'

I can't believe my ears—I'm going to Dunkirk tomorrow! And I'll be going once a week to have lessons at a real music academy. Monsieur Molin, you're my saviour! When I think how much whisky and Ricard and drivel you had to swallow! After two years of patient work and diplomatic skill, you finally succeeded in prising open the gates of my prison.

My mother takes me to the station and buys me first-class tickets, so I don't 'mingle', then she hurries home. I have to manage on my own and I have no idea how to get to rue Nationale. Luckily, Monsieur Molin is waiting for me at the station and he takes me to the academy. It's a big building that smells wonderful and is full of people saying, 'Hi! How are you?' There are students of every height and weight and with every sort of hair colour. It's beautiful, all these different people who look at ease with one another. The atmosphere in class is serious but cheerful: Monsieur Molin is a wonderful teacher; I'm very proud to have been accepted in his class and rather surprised nevertheless. Is this the dog-eat-dog jungle my father describes as the outside world? I'm also a little confused: why did Monsieur Molin fight so hard to get me here? He has plenty of other students who are much more interesting than I am.

Monsieur Molin still comes to the house for my piano and accordion tutoring. After lessons he makes sure I'm never with him when he goes to say hello to my father. I get the feeling he has a plan and is worried that having me there might cause it to fail. The next time, though, my father turns on the intercom and simply says, 'Come here.' When I arrive at the bar I see Monsieur Molin leaning on his crutches, his face inscrutable, and I fear the worst.

'The time has come,' says my father, 'for you to confront life's hardships. No more cocoon for you. Monsieur Molin has agreed to have you in Dunkirk three afternoons a week so you can study accordion and violin properly and improve your skills on the other instruments. You'll also have to start working: you'll spend all day Saturday as a salesgirl in Monsieur Molin's shop, and do the cleaning.'

It takes a tremendous effort to mask my enthusiasm. When Monsieur Molin has left, my father makes me sit down facing him and he explains that it's now time for me to start my mission in the world. I must marry; he'll take care of that. After six months he'll pay for me to divorce and I'll come back to live in the house. In the meantime, I mustn't get pregnant. I don't really understand but I agree, I accept everything unconditionally. He looks me in the eye for a long time, and I know it's vital that I don't betray my excitement, so I don't look away. I let him 'probe my mind' which is safely entrenched behind a wall lined with reflective mirrors—a recent improvement to my brick-wall technique.

Presumably in line with my father's plans for me, an extremely rare event occurs at home: my parents are paid a long visit by a mysterious stranger, then they call me into the living room. My father introduces me to a very small, thin, peculiar man; he must be in his fifties and speaks in a shrill and emphatically snobbish voice. While explaining in detail how much he likes ironing his little lace handkerchiefs, Monsieur Delataille examines me from head to foot, then quizzes me about Plato, Aristotle and the Italian Renaissance. He asks me what I think of Machiavelli, whether I like Impressionism…I tell him I do, I'm very impressionable. To my astonishment he even goes so far as to touch my hair!

After he has left my father summons me.

'It's time to think of marriage,' he tells me. 'A married woman can do everything she wants in life; she is always respectable. She can even get divorced, it doesn't matter. But you have to have been married.' Then he tells me about Monsieur Delataille: he's homosexual, rich and a Freemason. He too needs to be married, preferably to a pretty young girl, 'for the sake of appearances'. So he won't do me any harm and won't mind if I live with my parents most of the time.

I'm stupefied, speechless. I don't know what to think. Is this the biggest opportunity of my life, a chance to get out for real? Or am I risking being even more tied down if I marry my father's friend? I don't have to hesitate long because my mother intervenes forcefully: 'No!' she says. 'No, I don't agree to this. Maude can't marry a homosexual three times her age!' I look at her, stunned. It's the first time in my life I've known her to defend me and stand up to my father. Has this weird scheme stirred buried memories from the days when, as a little girl, she watched adults sealing her fate without considering her wishes? My father's reaction is even more surreal. 'Oh, well,' he sighs, and says no more about it.

An extraordinary victory. But such a bitter one! I'm grateful to my mother for flying to my rescue, but why did she wait such a long time? She could have tried to challenge his diktats long ago and she might have succeeded. I so needed her protection then...

But I'm still walking on air. I love taking the little train to Dunkirk, not that I travel first class as my father demands. I prefer going second class, where I sometimes meet up with a couple of railroad workers who have taken me under their wing and have even taught me how to play card games. They notice me looking up at each station, ready to jump out, and they say, 'There's no need to watch every stop like that, Dunkirk is the end of the line.'

On Sundays I help my mother work in the garden. If it rains we stay in the bar and have to endure long sessions on 'silence and impassibility'. My father explains that this is a way of 're-energizing' myself through contact with him after I've been contaminated by all sorts of pollutants outside. He never asks me about my life outside the house. In the evenings he waits for me so that we can eat a runny omelette swimming in burnt butter, and still insists we drink as much alcohol as he does. My mother and I sometimes manage to empty our glasses into the sink. During his 'teachings', my father now skips from one subject to another and is increasingly incoherent.

Every morning I work on studying for the *baccalauréat*. My parents didn't want to sign me up for the music *bac*, so I have to take the Latin and Literature exams again. I work alone; my mother refuses to exhaust herself on such a disappointing, ungrateful student. It's not easy but I stick at it and I try to use my experience from last year to study more intelligently. I haven't forgotten Abbot Faria's lesson: I have to do everything I can to go to university, my freedom depends on it. Of course, I go outside the gate almost every day now—something I couldn't even have imagined a few months ago. But that's only because my chain is longer, and not because I am truly free. How can I possibly settle for that?

With no help preparing for the exams, my results aren't brilliant and I fail my *bac* again. This time I dare to ask my father himself whether he will enrol me in a boarding school. I'm only seventeen and if I work hard I could pass my *bac* at eighteen. He tells me he has other, 'far bigger' plans for me, which fills me with dread. I have to face the facts: I won't realize my dream of studying medicine. I have no choice: I have to put all my energy into Monsieur Molin's solution. That is the route I must take to dig my tunnel to freedom.

The Santinas Jazz Band

It is incredible what Monsieur Molin has managed to get my
father to accept. I now work in his music shop every day, and join
the double bass class he teaches at the conservatory in Dunkirk.
My father agreed to this even though the classes are late in the
evening. I come home on the nine-thirty train, when it's dark and
there are sometimes drunken men in the carriage—I'm careful
never to mention them at home. Of course, I was given solemn
instructions: 'Now you're starting to complete your initiation into
the world. But be careful, I'll say this once again: you mustn't get
pregnant. Otherwise all my plans for you will fall apart.' Then
he warns me about 'sects', people who will try to persuade me
to go live with them; these sects are worse than religious groups
and their leaders are called gurus. The guru will make me take
drugs, which would wipe out all the training my father has given

me. Whenever my mother and I are alone, she comes back to this subject obsessively. She thinks I'm 'ideal prey' for sects because I'm weak, and she's terrified I won't be able to resist these gurus who have only one thing in mind: to get me into their beds.

It annoys me that she keeps coming back to the subject of sex. I have absolutely no desire to end up in anyone's bed. Anyway, I still feel very awkward and I hate my oversized body. Luckily I'm on friendly terms with Angèle, the young woman who runs the shop next door on the rue Nationale. She encourages me to try on clothes, explains which colours work together, the difference between fabrics, what a belt is, a scarf…Thanks to her, I now wear normal clothes, which has helped reconcile me somewhat to my appearance.

One Wednesday in December, halfway through a double bass lesson, the door opens and in steps a tall, very thin young man; almost the only thing visible above his thick red scarf is his black hair.

'Ah, here's tall Richard,' says Monsieur Molin. 'Come in.'

I've never seen anyone so tall or who looks almost as shy as me. Maybe his height is a burden to him too?

'What are you doing here, my friend?' Monsieur Molin asks.

Richard stammers that he's here for his Friday lesson.

'But it's Wednesday,' Monsieur Molin says with one of his winning smiles.

Richard opens his mouth and his cigarette falls to the floor. He bends down and makes a clumsy attempt to scoop up the ash.

'Here,' says Monsieur Molin, taking his arm, 'let me introduce you to young Maude, she's a great musician and so pretty too…'

I flush as red as Richard's scarf.

It turns out that Richard is twenty-five and has started studying double bass and solfège.

'I'm happy to see that someone at twenty-five still has the urge and the courage to take up a musical instrument,' says Monsieur Molin, and Richard's thin, introverted face suddenly lights up. I notice the way he looks at Monsieur Molin, as if he's gazing at the Messiah.

I immediately take a shine to this tall young man, and to his shyness and absent-mindedness. He sometimes comes to the music shop to buy strings and sheet music. He's the complete opposite of the sailors who follow me along the street, who confuse me with all their drivel and who are almost impossible to shake off. Richard hardly dares smile at me. He seems as much a novice, as much at a loss, as I am in everyday life.

When I get home in the evening I find my parents in exactly the same place I left them in the morning. I can't bring myself to ask my mother whether she spends her days holed up with him in the bar. My father now tries to spend as little time as possible in the house: as soon as his morning routine is over, we help him downstairs and he heaves a sigh of relief as he steps into the grounds. He doesn't go back to the house till bedtime; it's as if he's frightened of the big old place now. No one sets foot anymore in the large ground-floor rooms, where an atmosphere of deathly gloom pervades.

I can tell that my father views my work as a shop assistant and my double bass lessons as nothing more than a phase that he can put an end to at any time. I need to find a way to break out. Right now, though, I'm completely focused on the end of year exam that Monsieur Molin is determined I take at the conservatory.

After the trauma of the *bac*, I need all his encouragement before I agree to take it. Richard has promised to come and support me.

When the day comes, I perform a Bach *Chaconne*. My hands shake like leaves and my bow feels as if it's been greased with oil. I cling to somewhere deep inside me, rather as I used to during the alcohol exercises my father made me do. By the time I finish the piece, I'm dripping with sweat and I am filled with a strange feeling of unreality. Other pupils are waiting their turn with their parents, who encourage them, kissing their foreheads and even their hair. How wonderful that must be! Like an orphan, I clutch my bow, too much of a 'breed apart' to deserve a mother's love.

Monsieur Molin shakes me out of my stupor: 'My little one, you electrified the jury! You've won the conservatory's first prize. Congratulations! You really earned it.'

I smile, I'm pleased, but I wonder whether I really have earned it. I know that 'great musicians' play naturally: thanks to Madame Descombes, Monsieur Molin and the records I can now listen to, I know about real music, the sort of music that seems to reach for the skies. But for me music is synonymous with torture, suffering and hour upon hour of work. I have no spontaneity.

'What's the matter?' Monsieur Molin asks. 'Is something wrong?'

'I can't even improvise…'

'Well, little one,' he reassures me, 'contrary to what you might think, you can learn to improvise. You'll see when you come and play in my Santinas Jazz Band with me…'

My mother is worried about how frequently I am out of the house; she's convinced I'm 'seeing people' and that I'm in grave danger of falling prey to the first man to come along. Perhaps that's why my parents are in such a hurry to marry me off.

One day, when there's a public transport strike, Richard drives me home in his car. My mother asks him in and takes him to the bar, where my father is ensconced in his usual chair. He asks for Richard to be given a large glass of whisky and interrogates him about his age and his work. Then he asks my mother and me to leave the room. After a long private conversation, my father summons me back in and announces that Richard and I are to be married in three weeks' time, just long enough for the reading of the banns. The date is set for Saturday, July 24th. I'm speechless with surprise.

Lying in bed that night, I can't believe I'll be leaving the house for good to go and live with this painfully shy, handsome young man. Am I dreaming?

The Sunday before the wedding my father gives my mother and me an 'impassivity' exercise that I struggle to complete—I'm churning inside. Afterwards he asks my mother to leave us alone together.

'All these years have been devoted to moulding you,' he says. 'You're now entering an important phase, but first of all you need to have been married. So you're going to marry this young man but you won't consummate the marriage. Don't worry about dealing with that. In six months' time I'll pay for your divorce and you can come back to live here and accomplish your mission.'

I have to repress my shudders as I listen to his words. His voice grows still more solemn as he adds, 'Now, if you want me to let you go, you must promise that you'll come back in six months. If you refuse to promise you won't go.'

He tells me to raise my right hand and swear three times.

I raise my hand and I swear three times; at the bottom of my tattered heart I know for sure that I will break this oath. I will not get divorced after six months, I will not come back to live with him, I will not accomplish his 'great' mission. In fact, I will do everything I can to sustain my marriage and achieve my freedom.

On the Saturday morning of the wedding we perform his wake-up routine in silence. The last for me. My mother doesn't say a word; I realize with a heavy heart that she'll have to carry the chamber pot from now on; she'll be on her own here doing it. Then I take the little bag I've packed with a nightdress and two dresses bought from Angèle's shop. I slip my sticky-taped *Hungarian Rhapsody* into the bag along with *Notes from Underground,* which I stole from a box on the second floor. After all these years in this house, they are the only two things I want to take with me.

It's twenty to nine, and the ceremony is set for ten o'clock in the Dunkirk town hall. My parents won't be there. My mother accompanies me to the garden gate, where Richard has just parked. She lets me go without a word, without a kiss. Maybe it's better like this; if she opened her arms to me I think I'd bury myself in them. I'm dying to get away and yet I'm shaking with fear. The shutter at my father's window is open and I see the curtain move. He didn't say goodbye to me; he's hiding as he watches me leave. My heart constricts. I love my father and I miss him already. I hate my father and want to get away. As the gate closes behind me, the memory of my false promise feels like a blade driving through me. My mother is right: I can't be trusted. I'm leaving like a thief, like a traitor, like a rat off a sinking ship. I'm ashamed of myself, but I get into Richard's car and slam the door to erase the sound of the gate that first closed on me fifteen years ago.

I earn a living working full-time for Monsieur Molin. When we're confronted with a problem—a cranky customer, a tricky piano repair or the like—he says conspiratorially, 'Ah, my little Maude, the pair of us managed to get out of far more complicated situations, didn't we? We won't let a little problem like this stop us.'

For a long time now he has wanted me to play in the Santinas Jazz Band, a band in which all the musicians can play any of the instruments.

'Now that you're married you can come and rehearse with us in the evenings.'

I really like the four band members who play the trumpet, the double bass and the piano. But even though I can perform in front of professionals, I don't have it in me to play for a real audience. I feel as if I'd be putting myself in terrible danger: my father told me so many stories about dangerous crowds, like the mobs who throw rotten tomatoes at great opera tenors.

When performance day comes my stomach is in so many knots that I can't eat a thing. I've chosen dark clothes, in case I'm pelted with tomatoes. On the stage I cling to my double bass and play studiously while the other three musicians and Monsieur Molin on the banjo all seem to be enjoying themselves. The concert comes to an end and we leave the stage amid applause. Phew, we avoided the tomatoes! But what's happening? The clapping is getting louder, people are shouting, 'More!'

Monsieur Molin gives me a pat. 'Come on, little one, we're going back on.'

I panic slightly; I don't know what we're going to play, I don't have any more music prepared.

'Come on, guys,' Monsieur Molin says, 'let's give them "When the Saints Go Marching in".'

The audience are on their feet, clapping along. The band starts to let loose, clowning around. So it is possible to do things properly and to have fun at the same time. I gradually succumb to the excitement. I've never felt anything like it. I can feel my fingers softening over the strings, my body loosening, my face brightening and breaking into a smile all on its own. I wink at the trumpeter and he winks back at me!

It's wonderfully euphoric.

I'm not in a concentration camp. I'm not playing music to stay alive. I *am* alive. And I'm playing music for the pleasure of sharing the excitement with other musicians and other human beings.

I got out of my parents' house. I got out.

Epilogue

As a little girl, I used to make a promise to myself and seal it with a prayer: 'If I ever get out, I'll be in awe of everything I see. I pray that my father's voice will stay shut away in this house and won't follow me everywhere I go.'

I think I've kept my promise, but I sometimes wonder whether my prayer was answered. I often go to Arnhem Land in northern Australia, travelling deep into the bush with Indigenous Australians and staying with Max Davidson, a ranger who has been running a camp in this idyllic area for more than thirty years. The last time I was there, I dreamed I was staying in Max's wonderful place, surrounded by that beautiful country, which always gives me an intense feeling of freedom. Then the dream lens suddenly zoomed out, the magnificent scenery shrank dizzyingly before my eyes until it was a little model sitting on a table on the verandah in front of my father. He laughed: 'Ha, ha! To think that all these years she thought she was outside, when in fact she's never left the house.' My body stiffened with terror; I turned to look at Max, who nodded and said, 'Yes, I thought all this was real, too, but it was just a model.' I woke with a start.

Luckily, I don't have that dream very often, but it reminds me to remain vigilant. It has been thirty-eight years since I left my childhood home to get married. Then came the struggle to secure my emotional freedom. For a very long time, I couldn't talk about my past, not to my husband or my friends. Not even to my therapists. Whenever I did allude to my upbringing, I was always vague. Who could possibly have been interested? In truth, I was hiding my story like a shameful secret. I was afraid people would turn away. That they would look at me with disgust, the way Rémi did when he noticed my scar. I was terrified of ending up alone, again.

Mostly, I was so happy I'd escaped my imprisonment that I had no desire to go back, not even in my thoughts. I went to see my parents every week, with increasing discomfort, tormented by the guilt of having abandoned a sinking ship. My father eventually got used to Richard and stopped demanding that I divorce him. But as soon as I walked away, I would jump feet first into my 'real' life with 'real' people and 'real' relationships. I didn't have time to dwell on my past. It was much later that my buried fears emerged again, forcing me to confront the wounds of my childhood.

In the meantime, I had more urgent and far more exciting plans and longings. I wanted to walk for hours on end without being caged in by fences, to run on a beach that stretched to the horizon, to earn a living working with colleagues, to travel, to move furniture around, go into a bookshop and buy whatever book I wanted, listen to the Beatles, go to the cinema, laugh till I was breathless, cry freely.

Yet I had to learn the most basic codes for life in society: talking to strangers, finding my way in unenclosed places, eating in a restaurant with friends. It may seem obvious, but how do you eat, talk, drink, chew, reply and swallow at the same time without dribbling or choking? How do you pass someone on the footpath when there are people coming towards you? How do you say no? Or yes? I was too busy navigating all of this to dwell on the past.

It was only after my father died, in December 1979, that my body started to express the suffering I had buried. As soon as I was away from a professional setting where everything ran smoothly, I was gripped by muscle spasms, fainting fits, and episodes that I mistook for asthma attacks. I now realize these are all classic symptoms of what's known as Generalized Anxiety Disorder. I would clench my teeth and pull myself through with sheer willpower, just as my father had taught me. Besides, I was even less inclined to pay attention to these signs because I'd just given birth to a gorgeous green-eyed little girl. I kept repeating to myself: 'You got out, you're free.'

But being outside wasn't enough to make me free. I was still shut away behind the 'gates' of my upbringing: I felt guilty if I spent a single minute doing nothing; I always woke before my alarm and sprang out of bed without even taking the time to stretch; I planned my journeys so that I would get to meet-ings exactly at the appointed time, to the minute. I could feel unspoken fears from my childhood lurking in the dark forests of my mind, biding their time until they could pull me apart.

The fears leaped out at me the day I decided to change my life, to move away from the area and once and for all put some distance between me and my father's house. I was twenty-five. As I drove towards Paris, I had a panic attack that almost cost my daughter and me our lives. It was the first of many. On the surface, I was a highly effective construction lawyer. But underneath I was prey to the horrors experienced by other sufferers of panic attacks: nightmares that sent me straight back to the cellar seething with rats, where I was supposed to mingle with the dead; phobias that made the simplest tasks insurmountably difficult; debilitating obsessive-compulsive behaviour, rituals to 'protect me from the number three'; dizzy spells, fainting fits and panic attacks. My senses were constantly and terrifyingly in turmoil: pins and needles, dizziness, feeling of suffocation, a sense of imminent death…It was as if, by moving away from my father's house, I had inadvertently released the howling pack of wolves— my childhood fears.

At the same time, I started experiencing other physical side effects, some of them severe. I didn't see a dentist until I was eighteen, so my teeth were crumbling, my gums full of abscesses. My stooped back was prone to muscle tears as a result of the countless falls I had endured doing somersaults. The massive alcohol intake had irreparably damaged my liver, which secreted Gamma GT and transaminase enzymes as soon as it came into contact with substances as common as paracetamol. As for the scars on both sides of my body, doctors were baffled by them and swiftly dismissed my parents' explanation that they were 'left by an X-ray' or the result of a fall. To this day I don't know what caused them.

At a certain point I was so miserable that I no longer had a choice: I had to commit to some sort of recovery process. That was when I started my long journey with therapy, at the end of which I became a therapist myself. I did sometimes teeter on the edge of the abyss as I struggled to find the right kind of help. There was the Freudian analyst who saw me for a year and hardly spoke a single word: having suffered so much at the hands of silence, I felt I was being subjected to searing rejection all over again. Or another psychoanalyst who was besotted with puns and saw fit, at our first session, to assail me with: 'What do you know, it's Maude the Maudlin!' Or with the overly sensitive psychiatrist who was distraught by my story: he was convinced I was going to attempt suicide, and that I wasn't the sort to fail.

Until I finally met a warm-hearted female psychiatrist with whom I established a relationship of trust. It was again in books that I found my first real 'tools for life'. I read about the Palo Alto Mental Research Institute, where a movement of researchers revolutionized psychology and psychiatry by opening them up to other fields such as anthropology and sociology, and I started to find my way. My reading was its own form of therapy: it gave me the courage to reopen wounds I'd carefully concealed, to examine them calmly without picturing myself as a patient in the Bailleul mental asylum. Those researchers became my new companions, the way the heroes of novels had been in the past.

The birth of my second daughter was a great turning point in my life. I decided to start studying to become a therapist, so that I could help others find paths to freedom. Albeit by a convoluted route, I was pursuing the dream I'd cherished as a child, to be a 'surgeon of the head'. I threw myself passionately into psychopathology, the cognitive sciences and the study of hypnosis, studying in American, Canadian, then French universities, and training in a wide range of therapeutic approaches. My father wouldn't have been too happy: my methods were a perfect example of 'bad roots', refusing to bore down in one spot, instead jumping around from place to place.

As my studies progressed, I learned to control my panic attacks, anxieties and phobias. And yet my father's house still managed to sneak its way into my dreams every night: in a dream, out of nowhere, I'd cross the billiard room, or knock on my mother's bedroom door, or head to the bar. To stop these intrusions, I tried to 'build' my own castle, a place where, instead of being the prisoner, I would be the chatelaine. I created rooms to meet different needs or to resolve different mental blocks. That way I could allocate to each problem the most suitable tool, allowing it to work like a medicine implanted at the heart of the problem. Separate rooms also allowed me to isolate the different problems, as if behind fire doors, and stop them from contaminating each other.

This therapeutic technique, which I called the 'Castle Chronicles', was very useful later when I began helping others who, like me, had escaped someone else's psychological and emotional control. In this sort of controlling relationships, there is first a predator, an ogre who only cares about his own mental world, needs and urges. Other people are merely instruments or obstacles. The trap is set when a predator finds a victim. The ogre then gradually takes possession of the victim, all the while making the victim believe that this is love with a capital 'L', but also treating him or her as a contemptible wretch, whose sole value derives from the predator. The trap closes when the victim starts to identify with this debased image of him or herself.

The perfect example of a relationship of psychological and emotional control is the cult. But it would be wrong to think that all such relationships follow the mould of the guru with a horde of disciples. There are 'two-person cults', couples in which one consumes the other, or 'family cults' where the ogre is the mother or father, grandfather, grandmother; workplace hierarchies, distorted by a predator. Even some psychiatrists and personal-development coaches are ogres, and all the more destructive because they can abuse powerful therapeutic tools—such as hypnosis, which my father also used abusively—to enslave their patients and clients.

In my practice, I often gather the shipwrecked victims of these enslaving relationships. They are sent to me by concerned loved ones or doctors. Some are considered hopeless cases, but I know deep down that there is always a way out. I often tell my patients that freedom can flow through anything. Anywhere: seemingly menial acts, insignificant encounters, silly thoughts, minute gestures of resistance, tiny doses of progress. Anything and everything can be of help to fight controlling relationships.

The 'three-person family cult' of my childhood displayed virtually all the characteristics of a religious cult. My father, who warned me against gurus in the big wide world, was himself a guru incarnate. His encounter with the occult and his belief in 'spiritual powers' gave him a taste for domination, convinced him that he was a 'Chosen Spirit', and made him prepared to break common rules. Disappointed with life, he had turned his back on the 'fallen' world in favour of an increasingly delusional utopia. My mother was his first victim. He had made her dependent and incapable of resistance. He did not accord her the same rights as he had; to him she was nothing but a tool to serve his lofty ends: to bring me into the world and raise me. She experienced longings for rebellion, but didn't dare oppose her 'protector'. Any possibility of rebellion was nipped in the bud by the relentless and rigid system my father had set up.

Many decades later, my mother remains my father's victim. In cults, people side with the guru, even when they hate him. I think that my mother still probably believes in my father's theories, which makes her a 'willing follower'. This explains why we were never able to build a relationship. Today we are barely in touch with each other, although I still hope that she will come to terms with the fact that she is a victim. That's why I have dedicated this book to her.

And yet I eventually found my way to freedom. I was lucky enough to be given the unconditional love and tenderness of four wonderful animals: a dog, two ponies and a duck. And certain people—my first piano teacher, the frightened hairdresser, the high-school girl who failed her *baccalauréat*—also showed me friendship. Books and music opened my mind to ideas, feelings, and imaginary worlds that defied my indoctrination. As soon as I found a bit of courage, I constructed my own mental escape path, one stone at a time, using anything I could: inventing imaginary friends, digging a hiding place, writing forbidden stories and deliberately lying to exercise my autonomy. I was ready to grasp my saviour's hand when fate finally sent him my way: my music teacher, Monsieur Molin. He was a man of infinite goodness, who saw beauty in everything and was dazzled by life. He was the exact opposite of my father, and proof that my father was wrong: human beings are extraordinary.

ACKNOWLEDGMENTS

While writing this book, I returned to my childhood home for the first time in thirty years. I was shaken to discover it had been converted into an education centre for young girls, a sort of prison for delinquent minors. I would rather have seen it become a recreational facility or a vacation home...I was impressed, however, by the teachers' remarkable work—in both their educational and pastoral roles, by the way they worked alongside and encouraged their young wards. After the book came out, I returned once again to this house that was once my prison to give a talk: ironically the subject was freedom. My sincere thanks go to the teachers who welcomed me in and shared their experiences, especially to Marc and Séverine. And a heartfelt thank you goes to these young girls, for during the time I was able to spend with them I was touched by their beauty, curiosity and ability to appreciate the wonders of the world.

My profound gratitude to those I've met along my journey, some of whom remain unknown, who by a smile or kind look gave me the courage to persevere during difficult times. It's impossible to overstate how much a simple smile can change a life, and how one word or one aggressive look can darken the world.

Thank you to the people who have been by my side and continue to stand by me through my healing process. I cannot name them all; I will never forget the ways they showed their support and sympathy.

To André and Geneviève Molin, who left the gate part open and allowed me to slip out. To Henri Ibar and Sophie Ryckewaert, who gave the completely lost little girl that I was a chance at a professional life, who brought me to my first art exhibits, and invited me to a restaurant, where they showed me how to hold a knife and fork. To the musicians of the Santinas Jazz Band, who welcomed me into the band like one of their own. To Marc Julien, to whom I owe my first comic books, my first trips to the movies, and wonderful years together. To Marie-Jeanne, the first woman to hug me with maternal arms: in one fell swoop you melted the iceberg I thought I was trapped inside. To Jean, whose heart and eyes contain all the goodness of the world.

To the amazing doctors and therapists who provided me attention, commitment and kindness, and who are the reason I'm alive today: Dominique Verhaeghe, for telling me, 'Run, you have a life to live'; Jacques Pieri, for detecting the real wounds behind my physical suffering. Martine Bouvier, the first psychiatrist who got me to talk and who helped me open the doors to my internal prison; François Thioly, who taught me how to avoid falling into other controlling relationships.

To the excellent teachers I've been lucky enough to have and who had enough faith in me to include me in their working groups: Jeffrey Zeig, for teaching me that hypnosis can be used for the good to set someone free, and that getting better is a minute-by-minute job; Ernest Rossi, for introducing me to psychobiology; Steve de Shazer, who taught me how to connect music, emotions and therapy; Steve Andreas, who showed me the ethical dimension of neurolinguistics; John Gray, for teaching me how to bring a little humour into couple's therapy. Roger Solomon, my indefatigable teacher, EMDR supervisor and friend.

To Tony Robbins, who, a little over twenty years ago, was able to find the right words to show me what joy is. I am blown away by his unparalleled energy and the way he uses it to generate motivation and cheer. Like my father, he made me work hard, but, unlike my father, he focused on loosening my mental blocks, teaching me little by little how to free myself from guilt and take pleasure in the good things of life. When we ate together in Phoenix in 2004, I was able to measure the distance I've managed to come thanks to his support.

To Philippe Duverger, who taught me so much about adolescence. Marie-Rose Moro, who has helped me improve in the fields of psychopathology and therapy for fifteen years. Marie-Rose, you have a rare combination of precision, fairness and passion, and, as I keep telling you, you're a role model for me, both professionally and personally.

To the teaching teams so dear to my heart: those at the Faculty of Medicine at Paris XIII, at Cochin, at the Maison des Adolescents and La Maison de Solenn; the transcultural psychiatric team at Avicenne hospital, the team at the Milton-Erickson Institute in Phoenix.

To my study partners, George Kirschner and Marjorie, for encouraging me every time I was tempted to abandon my course in the United States.

To the people with whom I had so many fascinating conversations: Ron Davis, who, in the days when my speech was very impaired, never let me forget that a handicap can also be a gift; Annie Dumont, as well as being a friend, was a wonderful co-researcher in neuroscience; Trinh Xuan Thuan, who opened up the galaxy to me even if I still don't understand everything he says! Marilia Baker, for her enthusiasm and the time we spent with Elizabeth Moore Erickson; David Servan-Schreiber, whose friendship and our conversations I miss.

To my Australian friends, Deborah Rock and Rhys Jones, for introducing me to the struggles of Indigenous Australians; Max Davidson for his battle to stop Indegenous Australians being put into an enclosed space. The Aboriginal communities in Derby, Tichikala, Arnhem Land and Mount Borradaile, including Charlie, my 'skin brother', and Alexis Wright, who always says 'the fight is about believing the unbelievable', and who also believes that 'life flows through everything'.

To my patients, who each day share with me the most precious parts of themselves.

To you, Ursula Gauthier, my accomplice and fellow investigator in the labyrinth of my memories. You succeeded in opening doors deep inside me that I thought were sealed up forever.

To all the bookshops that I've so eagerly visited since I've been 'out' and who, with their advice, helped build my freedom. To the Parisian bookstore La Lettre Ouverte, which sadly no longer exists.

To my daughters, who turned me into a mother and gave me the strength to never give up. The world is more beautiful each day, thanks to you.

To my husband, my loyal companion who held my hand when my writing stirred fears from the past, and reminded me that I'm a happy woman now.

A special thank you to the animals in my childhood, who taught me to be a good human being, and to my four-footed friends, Twister and Trésor, who stayed patiently by my side while I wrote this book.

To dear Susanna Lea, thank you for bringing your light, your heart and your beautiful energy to this book. You truly are a ray of sunshine.

NOTE TO MY ENGLISH LANGUAGE READERS

I also owe many thanks to my English editors—Penny Hueston, Jean Garnett and Shadi Doostdar—and to you, my English readers. It is essentially thanks to you that a new chapter about my old struggle against manipulation has been opened, with a completely unexpected emphasis on...the English language. Though my level of English allowed me to take psychology classes at American universities, and even pass my exams, I have long struggled with a strange block preventing me from understanding a novel or film the moment it uses English. Words string together one after the next without making any sense, the plot completely escaping me. I become overwhelmed with panic, certain it's due to my own thorough stupidity, followed by an immeasurable sadness.

Through my studies in neuropsychology, I came to another

possible explanation. This inability could be attributed to the fact that as a child my ear was not trained to hear multiple voices or intonations. It was as if I suffered from a sort of selective cerebral deafness towards the sounds of language. Though I learned how to play numerous musical instruments, unfortunately that did nothing to improve my speech due to the brain's auditory zones for music being separate from those for spoken voice.

Knowing my book was going to be translated into English, I finally decided to confront my 'problem' with the English language. To be able to speak effectively about manipulation and control, one must be able to talk fluently with people, to feel what they've gone through, to understand intimately the 'story of their lives'. One cannot help others resist control by reciting theories or giving them a psychological evaluation.

This plan to improve my English, harmless in principle, ended up putting me through a year of hell such as I had not known in many, many years. Buried monsters stirred again and brought with them my old tendency to have paroxysmal nightmares. The same day I signed up for my first linguistic session in England, I dreamed my father was kicking me in the stomach. I was on the ground, and I could distinctly make out his pointy-toed shoe. The nightmares came back more and more frequently, even daily the week prior to my departure, and starting again once I returned to France. In other dreams, he would suddenly appear before me. In a cold gesture, he would move his hand across his throat as if he were cutting it. I awoke paralyzed and frozen with fear. This gesture, the cut throat, symbolizes the fate reserved for any traitor who revealed Masonic secrets.

They all came back to the surface, this string of similar

memories: the multiple oaths my father made me take throughout the years I lived behind the gate of his house. He would make me swear allegiance to the German language, the only language that maintained its original purity. On the other hand, I had to promise *never* to speak English, a 'denatured' language in its modern form, the usage of which could instil nothing but a 'leak of energy'. Though there was one exception: if I were to become a prominent figure, such as President of the United States or the director of a powerful organization like the Rockefeller Foundation, using English would be permissible only in so far as it advanced the ultimate goal 'to impose the use of German'.

In my head, these commands clashed with my father's express admiration for Americans, and the requirement he gave me of reading Shakespeare in the original language. But he could see no contradiction. He would tell me that the authentic English language had been 'lost' since Shakespeare, existing only in the initiation rites of certain English clubs. Extremely selective clubs—including among their members' ranks the Queen of England—that are the sole conservers of the 'pure language' faithful to its German roots.

Paradoxically, these nightmares helped me understand the origin of my strange inhibition regarding English. It did not come from 'thorough stupidity' or from a lack of exposure to the infinite diversity of voices. It stemmed directly from the commands my father had given a thousand times and the oaths I had to swear before him when I was just a child, while he made that terrifying gesture of cutting his throat. Only today can I decrypt the meaning of these incessant orders as: 'You will not speak English, under pain of death.'

As I struggle to overcome this conditioning, my body works against me. For months I have been suffering from a relentless bacterial infection ravaging my throat, my sinuses and my vocal cords, often resulting in a complete loss of voice. It's as if my body as an organism is saying psychosomatically, 'So you insist on speaking English? Ha! Not a single word will come out of your mouth.'

Recently, my nightmares took a turn for the worse: my father suddenly appeared before me, as if he was there but I hadn't seen him before. He placed his hand in front of his throat, watching me intensely. I struggled, but I wasn't strong enough, and my hand rose to my throat, my fingers turned sharp as razor blades, digging into my neck. Blood gushed forth while my hand reached deeper. My father said, 'You faltered.' Hopeless, I told myself I had failed, and felt my life slipping away.

One thing is certain: I was wrong to think the battle was over; I must struggle on. At night, my courage sometimes wavers beneath the weight of these nightmares. But I feel deep down that this is the final battle, and that I can be victorious. I am even more confident thanks to the exceptional people life has put in my path, each of whom has proved to be a valuable ally in this battle. Like Elaine and Patrick Tilley, a couple of professors at Oxford who hosted me for several days of linguistic immersion in their home. I fed off their expertise, their heartfelt kindness, and their home-made meals cooked with love. They have that mysterious ability to understand my story without knowing it, like Monsieur Molin once did. They opened up a new, safe space in their home that allowed me to fight my terrible nightmares and try to free myself from the command not to speak English.

Long after I had left my father's house, I continued to suffer sudden attacks of muteness, the after-effects of many years of confinement. With a great deal of effort, I had to learn how to master my elocution: articulating, pronouncing words with as much confidence as possible. Thirty years later, I was confronted with the same crises, this time involving the English language. I also had the pleasure of meeting Jeremy Coffman, who taught me patiently how to steady my breathing, stabilize my speech, and hone my pronunciation. For hours at a time while he was offering me wisdom in pedagogy and hearing, I often had the impression I was Colin Firth as Georges VI in the movie *The King's Speech*.

And, of course, I cannot forget Pol Heaney, a loyal friend who has helped me master the grammar, vocabulary and subtleties of this wonderful language, and my friend Charlotte Rachou, who is my irreplaceable bridge between the French and the English languages.